HOPE IS NOT A STRATEGY

HOPE
IS NOT A
STRATEGY

HOW GREAT LEADERS
BUILD REAL ACCOUNTABILITY

BRANDI NICOLE CHIN, PhD

HOUNDSTOOTH
PRESS

HOPE IS NOT A STRATEGY
How Great Leaders Build Real Accountability

FIRST EDITION

ISBN   978-1-5445-4998-9   *Hardcover*
          978-1-5445-4997-2   *Paperback*
          978-1-5445-4999-6   *Ebook*

CONTENTS

INTRODUCTION

Dear leader,

If you picked up this book, you're already doing more than most. You care about your people, about your work, and about getting it right. Let's be honest: If leadership were easy, more people would excel at it.

Here's what I've discovered over the last two decades: Even the best strategy, vision, or talent won't take you far without real accountability built in. Not the performative kind. Not the micromanaging kind. Real accountability.

I've seen organizations with all the right ingredients—funding, talent, strategy, passion—fall apart because they couldn't hold people to clear standards. This wasn't because they didn't want to, but because they thought they already were.

They assumed the follow-up would happen. They hoped people would do what they said. They believed that one moment of clarity was enough.

It wasn't.

The cost? First, the culture becomes unstable. Then, results dip. Confidence fades. Suddenly, that all-star team is missing goals, spinning its wheels, and wondering what went wrong.

I've coached leaders who mapped out brilliant plans but couldn't bring themselves to follow through when things got uncomfortable. I've worked with new leaders too scared to hold the line and veteran leaders too tired to continue the fight. The cycle remains consistent: good intentions, great vision, disappointing execution.

This doesn't have to be your reality.

The highest-performing leaders I've studied share these traits:

- They don't hope; they act.
- They don't wait for crisis; they prevent it.
- They build accountability from day one and never let it go.
- They make expectations unmistakably clear.
- They follow up consistently.
- They treat accountability as care, not punishment.

Accountability, done right, is a leadership multiplier. It amplifies your culture, unlocks performance, and builds trust. It's the difference between teams that talk about excellence and teams that live it.

Let me show you how I know this works.

I founded a school in Denver that became the highest-performing in the city in its very first year, achieving the highest academic growth in Denver and second highest in Colorado. It continues to thrive as one of the top-performing schools today.

Leaders flew in from across the country to discover our "secret sauce." After observing our morning meeting and advisory, I'd hear their whispered excitement. They'd ask, "How did you get hundreds of middle schoolers to read silently—and actually look happy doing it?" After roaming the classrooms and hallways, they'd gather and pepper me with questions, eager to understand how we made it all work.

I always shared everything I knew. But I gave fair warning first: "What I'm about to say isn't sexy. There's no magic bullet. In fact, you might find it…boring." I said this because people usually hoped for some fancy curriculum or shiny new initiative. That wasn't it. The truth was much simpler: I studied the very best in the field and became relentless about mastering the basics.

I learned from top performers in every area: recruitment, hiring, onboarding, adult culture, and student culture. I built classrooms that were joyful, rigorous, and safe. I visited schools across the country, learning from the top 1 percent of leaders and systems in their cities and states. I studied what they did, what they didn't do, and—most importantly—why.

This research created a playbook that led to exceptional, transformational results.

I also spent considerable time with leaders and schools that were mediocre—or failing entirely. These experiences were equally valuable. They taught me what to avoid and helped me recognize true excellence when I saw it, planned for it, and executed it.

Across all these observations—high-performing and low-performing schools alike—I noticed patterns. Many low performers had sound strategies and clear direction, but they lacked two critical elements:

1. precision in planning, and
2. a genuine system for accountability.

Regarding accountability, some thought they were implementing it effectively. Others left it to chance. The result was identical: inconsistency, frustration, and missed outcomes.

High performers demonstrated the opposite. Their planning was precise, and their execution was flawless. Accountability wasn't optional; it was embedded in their culture. They held themselves and their teams to the highest standards possible. The results were undeniable.

Two schools in the same neighborhood—sometimes even the same building—serving identical student populations could yield completely different results. The difference? Their approach to accountability.

For me, accountability was everything. No matter how comprehensive my playbook was—and it was comprehensive—I knew I couldn't succeed without it.

Years later, accountability became my true passion. If you had told me then I'd write an entire book about it, I would've been incredulous.

Two experiences changed that.

First, I began coaching hundreds of leaders across the US and internationally. The pattern was undeniable: Most had solid playbooks, but the leaders who thrived held their teams accountable. Those who didn't struggled. Accountability became the clear differentiator.

Second, this became deeply personal. I've always prioritized developing my team—especially my leadership team—because the investment pays dividends. As a successful real estate investor, I understand return on investment (ROI). Being a superhero leader might yield short-term results, but sustainable impact comes from building capacity in others. Both real estate and leadership are long games.

Investing in my leadership team became crucial to the secret sauce that visitors always asked about. It's why the school I founded continues to thrive today.

How does this relate to accountability?

I invested heavily in my leadership team. I modeled for them, planned with them, and observed alongside them, providing real-time feedback weekly, often multiple times per week. They became some of the best-trained leaders in the field. The strategy worked.

All of my leaders successfully led high-performing schools.

All except one.

Let's call her Sarah.

Sarah was the strongest instructional leader on my team. Her content knowledge exceeded even mine. She understood curriculum thoroughly and possessed the techniques to help students achieve mastery. Watching her teach was inspiring.

Yet, she struggled.

Several of her teachers weren't implementing her feedback. They didn't follow through. When we investigated the root causes, two issues emerged:

1. She lacked self-confidence, and
2. she struggled to hold people accountable.

We addressed these challenges. She identified her growth areas. I modeled; she observed. We analyzed my decisions: what I did, didn't do, and why. With my support and the strong culture we'd built, she eventually engaged those teachers effectively. Their results improved dramatically, and the entire school benefited.

She advanced to the assistant principal role. However, by then, I had stepped back. She reported to someone who didn't prioritize leadership development seriously. Although I had taught her everything I knew, when she became a principal in a different network, the results weren't consistent.

Now, in her third year as principal, her results are…inconsistent. There are pockets of success, but not the consistency or excellence we once achieved together.

What happened?

She still struggles to hold people accountable. She wants to be liked. She hopes that one conversation will create lasting change. When it doesn't, she becomes frustrated. Despite all our work together, the accountability mindset didn't take hold.

This gap—between knowing and doing, between strong ideas and strong follow-through—is exactly why this book exists.

I wrote this book because I've watched talented leaders

fall short—not due to lack of effort, but due to lack of follow-through. Clarity without accountability is just conversation. The kind of leadership our organizations deserve demands courage, not comfort.

Most importantly, accountability done right isn't harsh; it's transformative.

WHAT THIS BOOK WILL DO FOR YOU

This book is designed for leaders who want real results, not just inspiration, but implementation. This book is written primarily for education leaders: superintendents, network leaders, principals, and anyone responsible for driving results in schools. If you're leading outside of education, you'll find that these principles translate powerfully to any organization where culture, clarity, and follow-through matter.

We'll cover essential concepts and mindsets, but more importantly, you'll gain practical tools. You'll receive actionable steps and resources you can apply immediately. Whether you're leading a team of two or two hundred, you'll develop the structure and knowledge needed to build accountability into your culture's foundation, so your team delivers with clarity, consistency, and ownership.

You'll also learn how to:

- Transform accountability from a source of stress into a leadership advantage
- Navigate the common pitfalls that trap even seasoned leaders in mediocrity
- Integrate accountability into your team's daily operations—without micromanaging
- Build a culture founded on commitment, not compliance

If you've ever struggled to drive execution, felt frustrated by repeated underperformance, or hesitated to hold people accountable due to fear of pushback, or if you're simply ready to elevate your leadership, this book is for you.

Let's begin.

PART 1

WHY ACCOUNTABILITY MATTERS

CHAPTER 1

ACCOUNTABILITY IS NOT A DIRTY WORD

"Clear is kind. Unclear is unkind."
—BRENÉ BROWN

Accountability.

Just hearing the word might make you wince a little.

The very word conjures visions of awkward conversations, dreaded meetings, and those dreaded performance evaluations. But what if accountability wasn't something to fear? What if, instead of being a source of stress, it became the key to unlocking performance, trust, and excellence within your organization?

That question came to life for me during a recent training I led with a group of school and network leaders. I asked them, "What words or feelings come to mind when you hear the word accountability?" Like any good educator, I gave them think time.

After a minute or so, the responses started rolling in, and I wrote each one on chart paper at the front of the room.

"I'm in trouble." "Mean." "Micromanage." "Bad at my job."

Now, if that's what leaders are thinking, imagine what teachers and staff are carrying.

The problem isn't the word. It's the experience. Most of us have only seen one version of accountability: the one that feels top-down, punitive, and fear-based. That version gets enforced on people, not built with them.

But accountability isn't inherently negative. There are two kinds.

One that enforces compliance. And one that empowers ownership.

We're all familiar with the first. But the second—the one grounded in clarity, trust, and shared responsibility—is what this book is about. To use accountability as a tool for growth, we have to reframe what it means and how it's done.

Close your eyes. Imagine a workplace where everyone knows what's expected of them, feels supported in meeting those expectations, and views feedback as a tool, not a threat. That's accountability done right.

It's not about blame. It's not about micromanagement. It's about clarity, consistency, and culture.

And it applies everywhere: in elementary schools, high schools, charter networks, district offices, and really any organization where results matter. Accountability is the foundation of every high-performing organization.

So if it's that important, why is it so hard to get right?

WHY ARE LEADERS SO AFRAID TO HOLD THEIR TEAMS ACCOUNTABLE?

Because accountability is personal.

Leaders fear that if they push too hard or follow through

too directly, they'll send the message that someone isn't good at their job. And no one wants to be that leader. Add the pressure of staff retention, the desire to keep team morale high, and the discomfort of hard conversations—and suddenly, holding the line feels risky.

The reality is this: Skipping accountability doesn't protect people; it confuses them. It doesn't build loyalty; it erodes trust. And it doesn't retain talent; it drives your best people out the door.

FEAR OF LOSING STAFF

Many leaders hesitate to hold their teams accountable because they fear losing employees in an already competitive talent market. The worry is understandable; retention is a challenge, and leaders don't want to risk pushing good people out.

But here's the truth: If someone leaves your team because you held them accountable to agreed-upon expectations, then they weren't the right person for your team in the first place. And contrary to what many leaders assume, accountability doesn't drive people away; it keeps the right people in. Research shows that teachers in schools with strong accountability structures are 50 percent more likely to stay than those in schools where expectations are unclear.

Mission-driven people who care about doing great work don't run from accountability; they demand it. High performers hold themselves accountable and thrive in environments where growth is prioritized, feedback is clear, and excellence is expected.

Nothing frustrates a great employee faster than watching low performers coast by with no consequences. When leaders fail to enforce high standards, they don't just keep underperformers; they drive away the ones who actually care.

When you build a culture of accountability, you don't push great people away; you attract and retain them. By holding everyone to high expectations, you create an environment where the best thrive, and those who aren't aligned naturally exit. And that's exactly what you want.

THE DESIRE TO BE LIKED

Alicia had just stepped into her dream role: executive director of a youth-serving nonprofit she deeply believed in. The staff was small, tight-knit, and passionate. Most had been there longer than she had, and from day one, Alicia felt the pressure to prove she belonged. So she made what felt like the safe choice: She focused on being liked.

She praised publicly, avoided giving critical feedback, and extended deadlines without asking questions. When staff missed key deliverables, she covered for them. When a team member pushed back in meetings, she let it slide. "I didn't want to come off as controlling," she told a colleague. "I thought if I gave people space, they'd respect me more."

But that's not what happened.

Within months, clarity gave way to confusion. Norms became optional. One project fell behind. Then another. High performers started pulling away, frustrated that they were carrying the load. Alicia could feel it: People were smiling in meetings but quietly doing their own thing. A longtime staffer eventually left, saying they didn't feel supported or held to a shared standard.

That's when it clicked. Trying to be liked had cost her what she actually needed: trust. Not because she wasn't kind, but because she wasn't consistent.

Leadership is relational, and it's easy to confuse accountability with conflict. Many leaders believe being agreeable or avoiding confrontation will make their staff like them. But let's get real: Being liked isn't the goal of leadership; being respected is.

Respect is earned when you follow through on what you said you would. And you can't do that without holding yourself and your team accountable. The irony? What leaders fear will damage relationships—honest accountability—is actually what strengthens them. Real trust is built on clarity, fairness, and follow-through.

WHAT ACCOUNTABILITY REALLY IS

Many leaders misinterpret accountability as being synonymous with punishment or micromanagement. They worry that enforcing standards will make them seem harsh, rigid, or controlling. The hesitation is real. But here's the truth: When accountability is done right, it doesn't create fear; it builds trust.

Accountability isn't about catching people slipping. It's about creating clarity, offering support, and reinforcing what matters most. It's the structure that helps people succeed, not the spotlight that exposes failure.

When expectations are clear, feedback is timely, and follow-through is consistent, people feel safe. They know where they stand. They know you're paying attention. That's not control; that's leadership. The absence of accountability, on the other hand, breeds confusion and frustration. It's not neutral. It creates a slow drift toward mediocrity, and your strongest people will feel it first.

WHAT'S AT STAKE WHEN YOU DON'T HOLD YOUR TEAM ACCOUNTABLE?

A lot. Leaders who fail to build accountability into their organizations don't just see missed deadlines and sloppy execution; they create a culture of uncertainty, frustration, and decline. The consequences of weak accountability ripple across an entire team, leading to:

- **Missed Goals:** Without consistent follow-up, projects stall, deadlines slip, and key initiatives never gain traction.
- **Low Morale:** When expectations are enforced inconsistently, resentment builds among those who do their jobs well.
- **Lost Talent:** High performers refuse to work in environments where mediocrity is tolerated, so they leave.
- **Damaged Credibility:** Leaders who don't hold their teams accountable lose respect, making it harder to inspire, influence, and drive change.
- **Culture Decay:** Over time, an organization without accountability erodes from within, making recovery difficult and costly.

The most dangerous part? These consequences often happen slowly—so slowly that leaders don't realize how much ground they've lost until it's too late. Accountability isn't just about short-term performance; it's about long-term sustainability.

BUILDING A CULTURE THAT EMBRACES ACCOUNTABILITY

When I became a founding principal at a middle school—a school that would go on to become one of the highest-performing in the city—we hosted countless visitors on what we called "excellent school visits." Leaders, founders, and educators would come to observe our classrooms, talk to our teachers, and try to understand what made our school so successful. Inevitably, someone would pull me aside and ask, "What's your secret?"

Most assumed I'd say something about test prep strategies, extended day schedules, or incentive systems. What they didn't expect was to hear me talk about rubrics, morning huddles, and the magic of doing the most basic things ridiculously well.

"This story is about the most thrilling part of education," I used to joke. "Classroom entry routines!"

I get it. On the surface, it sounds boring. But stay with me.

When I started, I faced a harsh reality: My team averaged just 1.1 years of experience compared to 7.1 years at other successful schools. I couldn't rely on seasoned expertise; I had to build it. That meant coaching and development would have to be the engine. But coaching only works in a culture that embraces feedback, not just tolerates it.

It was the summer before our first school year, and my team was gearing up for what we called our "Strong Start"—a carefully choreographed launch that set the tone for culture, instruction, and accountability. Every minute of the first two weeks was intentional, and it all hinged on one deceptively simple concept: clarity.

"The first two weeks of school are where you win or lose the year," I told my team. "If teachers don't know what 'good' looks like—and if they don't believe we'll hold the line on it—we lose credibility before the first quiz is even graded."

So we built what we called "the first-ninety-day playbook." It wasn't flashy, but it was bulletproof.

We started with classroom expectations, every single one of them. From the first five minutes of class to the last, we mapped out teacher moves, student behaviors, and systems. We didn't just name them. We turned them into rubrics.

There was a rubric for the Do Now. A rubric for how students entered the classroom. Indicators for how materials were passed out, where homework was written, and even how quiet "quiet" actually had to be. On the left side of each rubric: clear teacher actions. On the right: clear student behaviors. No secrets, no surprises.

And most importantly, every leader and teacher practiced them. During summer professional development, teachers didn't just sit through PowerPoint slides; they role-played classroom entry like it was Broadway. Leaders and peers scored each other using the rubric. Non-examples were dramatized with flair. (Shout out to Ms. Rivera's Oscar-worthy "late-to-class student" performance.) We turned what could've been tedious into something memorable—and even fun.

We told teachers, "You'll know exactly what we're looking for. We're not hiding the ball. We'll even tell you what day we're coming—and what we're looking for when we do."

Each day, leaders observed classrooms for specific "taxonomy skills," the exact moves outlined in the rubrics. We tracked proficiency and shared the school's progress during quick, twenty-minute daily huddles. Teachers got feedback, celebrated wins, practiced again, and kept going.

And we had a school-wide goal: 80 percent of classrooms proficient in a subset of taxonomies within the first two weeks of school.

We made the goal loud and clear. It wasn't hidden in a spreadsheet. Everyone knew where we were each day. We shouted out teachers who crushed it, and we celebrated growth, even when it was small.

By day ten, we hit the 80 percent mark, and then some. There were still two school days left in the launch window. The system had worked. Not because it was groundbreaking. Not because it was tech-enhanced. But because it was clear, practiced, and reinforced.

People think clarity is boring. But I'll tell you, it's the most energizing thing in the world when you do it right. It builds confidence. It builds momentum. And it makes people feel like they're part of a winning team.

So yes, this is a story about classroom entry routines. But more than that, it's a story about what's possible when you make success so clear, people would have to try to get it wrong.

I also built the feedback culture from the ground up. Feedback wasn't a sidebar or an annual formality; it was the heartbeat of our school. I embedded it into our hiring process, assessed for it in interviews, and made it a condition of staying on the team. We used a simple test: During interviews, we gave real-time feedback on teaching demonstrations and watched how candidates responded. Did they lean in? Get defensive? Could they actually implement the change? This told us everything about whether they could thrive in our culture.

The result? We became the highest-performing school out of 203 in our first year, and we've maintained that excellence. Not because we had the most experienced team, but because we had the most accountable one.

You can't have quality without consistency, and you can't have consistency without accountability. Coaching ensures quality. Accountability ensures everyone does the work. One without the other falls short of transformation.

MAKING FEEDBACK WORK: THE EMOTIONAL SIDE OF ACCOUNTABILITY

Here's what I learned the hard way: Accountability almost always includes feedback, whether through data, coaching conversations, or performance reviews. And while many leaders focus on what needs to be said, they underestimate how it lands emotionally.

In my school's first year, when interim data showed we were second to last in math, I presented it straightforwardly to my team. I expected urgency and energy. Instead, I got tears. Some teachers took it personally. Others shut down completely. I had no plan for managing the emotional weight of the moment.

That's when I realized: Data is feedback. And feedback is triggering—period. According to *Thanks for the Feedback* by Douglas Stone and Sheila Heen, there are three primary triggers that shape our reactions:

1. **Truth Triggers:** "That's not accurate" or "They don't understand"
2. **Relationship Triggers:** "I don't trust who's giving this feedback"
3. **Identity Triggers:** "This challenges how I see myself"

Understanding these triggers changed how I delivered feedback forever. I learned to anticipate emotional reactions, frame feedback as a growth opportunity, and follow up to ensure it stuck.

TWELVE MINDSET-SHIFT STRATEGIES FOR LEADERS AND TEAMS
WHAT LEADERS CAN DO FOR THEMSELVES

- ✓ **Reframe Your Language:** Replace "I hate giving negative feedback" with "Feedback is a gift that helps us grow." Replace "This will be uncomfortable" with "This is an opportunity for improvement."
- ✓ **Normalize Feedback for Yourself:** Ask your team regularly: "What's something I can do better?" Show that feedback is part of your growth, not a threat to your authority.
- ✓ **Model Receptiveness:** When someone offers feedback, don't defend; get curious. Respond with: "That's helpful. Can you say more about what you noticed?"
- ✓ **Plan for Emotional Reactions:** Before the conversation: Anticipate possible reactions. During: Pause if emotions rise. After: Follow up to reinforce the feedback.

WHAT LEADERS CAN DO FOR THEIR TEAMS

- ✓ **Normalize Feedback as Culture:** Use the phrase "Around here, feedback is a normal part of how we grow." Include feedback norms in onboarding and team meetings.
- ✓ **Create Psychological Safety:** Make it clear that feedback is about the work, not the person. Use sentence starters like, "I'm sharing this because I care about your growth and success."
- ✓ **Foster Peer Accountability:** Create shared agreements and ask the team to hold each other to them. Celebrate when

team members support one another through honest, helpful feedback.

✓ **Coach on Feedback Triggers:** Introduce the three trigger types and ask, "Which trigger tends to show up for you most?" Role-play tough feedback moments to build resilience.

✓ **Highlight How Top Performers Grow from Feedback:** Share stories of respected team members who adjusted and grew after receiving feedback. Invite experienced staff to talk about their own learning curves. Make growth stories part of your culture narrative, not just performance celebrations.

FROM MINDSET TO METHOD: INTRODUCING THE VERB FRAMEWORK

Shifting your mindset around accountability is essential—but mindset alone isn't enough. You need a systematic approach that turns these principles into practice. You need a framework that helps you build accountability consistently, regardless of your school context, team size, or experience level.

That's where the VERB framework comes in.

Over the next four chapters, you'll learn how to implement accountability through four interconnected elements:

- **Values First:** Establishing the foundation that drives all decisions
- **Expectations Clear:** Creating crystal-clear standards everyone understands
- **Real Progress:** Tracking and measuring what matters most
- **Buy-In and Ownership:** Building commitment that drives results

Each element builds on the last, creating a comprehensive system for accountability that feels empowering rather than punitive. By the end of Part 2, you'll have the tools to transform accountability from a source of stress into your greatest leadership advantage.

The mindset work we've done in this chapter matters—but now it's time to put it into action.

CHAPTER 2

THE VERB FRAMEWORK

YOUR ROADMAP TO RESULTS

> *"You do not rise to the level of your goals. You fall to the level of your systems."*
> —JAMES CLEAR, *ATOMIC HABITS*

By now, you've done the hardest work: shifting your mindset around accountability. You understand it's not about punishment or micromanagement. You know it builds trust rather than destroys it. You've even started planning for those emotional reactions that used to derail your best intentions.

But mindset alone won't get you there. You need a system.

Here's the secret most leaders miss: Accountability isn't complicated, but it is systematic. The leaders who get it right aren't winging it or hoping for the best. They're following a simple, repeatable process that keeps their teams aligned and performing at their highest level.

The problem? Too many leaders reduce accountability to a single moment: a tough conversation, a formal write-up, or a last-ditch meeting when things have already gone sideways. But real accountability isn't about crisis management. It's about the system you build every single day, in every interaction, through every decision you make as a leader.

That's exactly what the VERB framework is designed to do. It transforms accountability from something you dread into something your team expects—and thrives on.

INTRODUCING THE VERB FRAMEWORK

The VERB framework breaks accountability down into four essential components—simple, actionable, and designed to work in the real world, not just in theory. Think of it like scaffolding: You need all four corners for the structure to stand.

Here's the framework:

V—Values First

E—Expectations Clear

R—Real Progress

B—Buy-In and Ownership

V.E.R.B. ACCOUNTABILITY FRAMEWORK

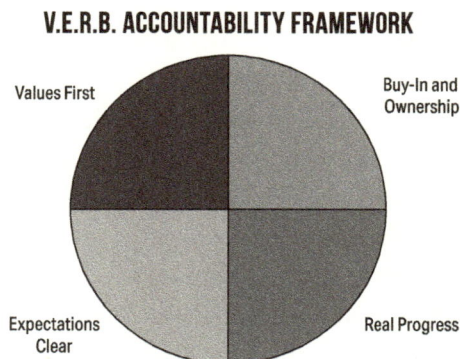

Values First

Buy-In and Ownership

Expectations Clear

Real Progress

But here's the catch: It only works when all the components are present. A common pitfall is that leaders latch on to one part—like setting expectations or offering support—and ignore the rest. That's like trying to drive a car with one wheel. Each part reinforces the others. Skip one, and the whole system wobbles.

Let me show you how each piece works, and why they're more powerful together than apart.

VALUES FIRST: THE FOUNDATION THAT DRIVES EVERYTHING

Most organizations have values posted somewhere: on walls, on websites, or in employee handbooks. But having values and living values are two very different things. Values First means defining what matters most and then anchoring every expectation, every decision, and every conversation to those shared principles.

This isn't about crafting perfect mission statements. It's about clarifying what those values look like in action—so your team doesn't just name them, they live them.

Example: If "collaboration" is a core value, don't leave it to interpretation. Spell out exactly how it shows up: shared planning time every Tuesday, transparent communication through weekly updates, rotating facilitation during team meetings, and support protocols when someone is struggling. When values are vague, they become meaningless. When they're specific, they become powerful.

Values First also means you use these principles to make decisions when things get complicated. When a team member pushes back on feedback, when deadlines get tight, when personalities clash, your values become the North Star that guides your response. Without this foundation, accountability feels arbitrary. With it, accountability feels fair and consistent.

EXPECTATIONS CLEAR: MAKING SUCCESS INEVITABLE

Here's where most leaders think they're being clear, but they're not. Setting expectations isn't just about naming goals or assigning tasks. It's about creating conditions where success is almost inevitable because everyone knows exactly what they're aiming for and how they'll get there.

Expectations Clear means four things:

Set measurable, nonnegotiable goals that come with a compelling "why." Not just "improve student engagement" but "85 percent of teachers will use engagement strategies daily because engaged students learn more and feel more connected to school."

Backward-plan milestones using a detailed implementation calendar. Break big goals into two-week sprints with specific checkpoints, so you're course-correcting early instead of scrambling late.

Define roles clearly so every leader knows who's owning what—and when. No more "I thought you were handling that" moments that derail progress.

Establish success criteria through rubrics or clear indicators that spell out exactly what excellence looks like for everyone involved. Remove the guesswork.

Make consequences transparent up front so there are no surprises when someone gets off track. This isn't about threats; it's about clarity.

Example: You're implementing new engagement strategies across your team. Instead of hoping people figure it out, you set a goal (85 percent daily implementation), create a timeline (week one: training, week two: practice with feedback, week three: full implementation), assign specific leaders to conduct daily walk-throughs, develop a rubric that defines what "engagement strategies" actually look like in practice, and establish that teachers not meeting the standard will receive additional coaching and support. No winging it. No confusion.

REAL PROGRESS: TRACKING WHAT MATTERS

This is where accountability gets real. Real Progress means you're not waiting until the quarterly review or annual evaluation to see how things are going. You're tracking progress visibly and often, making data review and feedback part of your weekly rhythm.

It's the difference between hoping things are working and knowing they are—or knowing exactly where to intervene when they're not.

Real Progress looks like leader check-ins every week, dashboards that everyone can see, and responding in real time when someone gets off track. When you spot a problem, you don't wait; you act.

Example: A teacher is struggling with the new engagement strategies. Instead of scheduling a meeting "sometime next week," you walk into the conversation prepared. You have observation notes from three different walk-throughs, specific examples of what you've seen, and clear next steps that you've already discussed with your manager. The conversation sounds like, "Based on what we've observed this week, here are the specific areas where you're on track and here's where we need to focus. I'm going to co-plan with you on Monday and observe again Tuesday so we can see your progress together." Clarity is the antidote to confusion—and to drift.

This isn't micromanaging; it's managing. When people know you're paying attention and that you'll follow through on support, they perform better. When they know problems won't fester, they trust the system.

BUY-IN AND OWNERSHIP: MAKING ACCOUNTABILITY SHARED

The final piece is often the most overlooked, and it's why so many accountability systems fail. Buy-In and Ownership means accountability doesn't feel like something that's being done to your team. It feels like something they're part of creating and sustaining.

This is where you address resistance both publicly and privately, celebrate wins loudly and specifically, and use stories, data, and visuals to keep momentum high. People need to see that the system is working, and that they have agency within it.

Example: You send daily emails that spotlight specific progress and shout out bright spots. At your weekly team meeting, you share photos of student engagement, include student voices about what's working, and display a progress tracker that shows how the whole team is doing. You ask team members to share what's working in their classrooms and how they're supporting colleagues. When someone struggles, the team rallies to help instead of watching from the sidelines.

Buy-In and Ownership also means creating space for people to have input on how accountability happens. They might not get to decide whether expectations exist, but they can help shape how progress gets measured or how support gets delivered. When people feel heard and involved, resistance drops and ownership rises.

WHY ALL FOUR COMPONENTS MATTER

Each piece of the VERB framework builds on the others. Values without clear expectations feel inspiring but vague. Clear expectations without progress tracking feel like wishful thinking. Progress tracking without buy-in feels punitive and top-down. And buy-in without values feels superficial and short-lived.

But when you put all four together, something powerful happens:

- Excuses disappear because everyone knows what's expected and why it matters.
- Trust builds because the system is transparent and consistent.

- Performance improves because people get the support they need when they need it.
- Culture strengthens because accountability becomes something the team owns together.

The leaders I've worked with who master this framework don't spend their time chasing people down or having crisis conversations. Their teams self-correct, support each other, and push themselves because they believe in what they're building.

YOUR NEXT STEPS

Over the next four chapters, we'll dive deep into each component of the framework. You'll see exactly how to identify and operationalize your values, how to set expectations that actually drive behavior, how to build progress-tracking systems that inform rather than overwhelm, and how to create buy-in that makes accountability feel empowering rather than imposed.

But here's your charge right now: Stop trying to fix accountability with piecemeal solutions. Stop hoping that one great conversation or one new policy will solve everything. Start thinking systematically.

Because when you build the full VERB framework, accountability stops being something you enforce and becomes something your team embraces. And that's when real transformation begins.

PART 2

IMPLEMENTING THE VERB FRAMEWORK

CHAPTER 3

VALUES FIRST

Values are the foundation of accountability. Without clearly defined values, accountability becomes an exercise in compliance. What you're left with is simply a set of rules—and rules aren't inspiring.

However, when values are explicit and shared, they act as the standard by which actions, decisions, and outcomes are measured. Accountability is how an organization protects what it says it cares about. If a school or team claims to value equity, excellence, or urgency, then it must create structures to regularly assess whether those values are showing up in daily practice—and address it when they're not.

In short: Values define what matters. Accountability ensures it actually happens.

THE PROBLEM: VALUES THAT LIVE ONLY ON WALLS

When it comes to Values First, most organizations think they've got it covered. They've got their values named, printed on T-shirts, displayed proudly on their websites, and maybe even hanging in the lobby. But here's where they fall short: Values are more than just words; they need to be put into action.

Naming values isn't enough. Many organizations stop there; they don't take the next crucial step of defining what those values look like in action. If you can't define what those values look like in practice, you can't expect your team to live them—or hold anyone accountable to them.

Let's take "respect," for example. It's one of the most common values you'll find in organizations, but what does it actually mean?

I've led countless leadership sessions where I've asked a simple question: "How do you define respect?"

Every single time, I get a different answer. One person says, "It means saying please and thank you." Another says, "It means being honest, even when it's hard." Someone else offers, "It means not interrupting in meetings."

All valid. All totally different. And that's a problem.

If everyone in your organization has a slightly different definition of respect, how do you expect them to embody it the same way? How do you hold people accountable when the meaning isn't clear? The short answer is: You won't.

THE SOLUTION: DEFINE YOUR CORE VALUE BEHAVIORS

Strong organizations don't just name their values; they define the behaviors that bring them to life. These are your core value behaviors (sometimes called operating principles). They're the actions that tell your team exactly what living the value looks like.

For example, a school that names "equity" as a core value might define it through a behavior like "We disaggregate data by student group and adjust instruction in real time." A real estate team that values "responsiveness" might say, "We respond to every client inquiry within twenty-four hours, even if just to share a timeline for a full answer."

This approach to defining and operationalizing core values was refined during my time at Denver School of Science and Technology (DSST) Public Schools under the leadership of CEO Bill Kurtz. Under his guidance, DSST became nationally recognized not only for academic excellence but for building exceptional organizational culture, earning recognition as one of Denver's Best Places to Work year after year. The values operationalization process became a cornerstone of how the network sustained both high performance and strong culture at scale.

Here's how to define (or refine) your core value behaviors:

1. START WITH YOUR LEADERSHIP TEAM

If leaders aren't clear and aligned on what your values look like in action, the team won't be either. Have everyone work individually first, then come together to create a unified list of behaviors that align with each value. Work through these questions together:

- What does this value look like in action?
- What does it sound like in conversation?
- How do we model this daily?
- Where are we strong? Where do we fall short?
- How should people feel when this value is consistently upheld?
- What behaviors might be confused with this value but actually don't reflect it?

2. ENGAGE THE FULL TEAM

Have your team weigh in—because people buy into what they help build. Repeat this exercise with your full staff. Include your leadership team as participants to ensure the behaviors defined at the leadership level align with how the larger team operates.

You'll likely end up with a long list of potential behaviors, so plan for multiple rounds of narrowing. Use strategies like dot voting, small group sorting, or prioritizing based on impact to identify the three to five behaviors per value that matter most.

3. WRITE IT DOWN AND MAKE IT OFFICIAL

Once your values and core behaviors are clear, codify them. Turn them into a commitment. Whether it's a signed document, a pledge, or a shared agreement, make it something everyone actively commits to upholding. Accountability starts with clarity.

Here's what that can look like in practice, using a real example from my founding school at DSST. You'll see the network values on the left and how my leadership team and I defined them with our staff on the right:

CORE VALUE	CORE VALUE BEHAVIORS (OPERATING PRINCIPLES)
Respect	Listen mindfully to understand others' views
	Intentionally call out successes
	Show gratitude and appreciation
	Go directly to the source—no gossip
Courage	Speak up and voice your opinion
	Step outside your comfort zone
	Hold teammates accountable
	Engage in healthy conflict; don't avoid it
Doing Your Best	Prepare and practice ahead of time
	Actively solicit feedback (good to great)
	Respect each other's time: Start/end meetings on time
	Avoid distractions and stay fully engaged
Integrity	Do what's right, not just what's easy or popular
	Follow through: Say what you mean; mean what you say
	Be truthful, honest, and own your actions

CORE VALUE	CORE VALUE BEHAVIORS (OPERATING PRINCIPLES)
Responsibility	Complete your part of the whole
	Name and own your mistakes
	Meet deadlines and stay timely
Curiosity	Ask to understand before assuming
	Own your learning: Seek growth without waiting for professional development (PD)

MAKING VALUES VISIBLE AND MEMORABLE

Don't stop at documentation; post your values everywhere. Put them on the walls, in agendas, in team huddles, and on your Slack channel. The goal isn't decoration; it's repetition.

Neuroscientist John Medina reminds us to "repeat to remember." Visibility isn't just about aesthetics; it's a memory strategy. Repetition strengthens recall, especially when the values are revisited frequently and in multiple formats. When values are visible, they become usable. They stop being abstract ideals and start becoming embedded habits—because what the brain sees often, it remembers.

Visibility keeps values top of mind and signals that they're not just words—they're how we work.

THE COST OF UNSPOKEN EXPECTATIONS

When we don't make values and expectations visible, the cost can be steep. Let me tell you about Jasmine.

Jasmine had just been promoted from principal to chief schools officer. It was the summer before the new school year, and she was responsible for supporting five schools, all of which were gearing up for intensive summer training. The pace was fast, the stakes were high, and she dove straight into execution mode. There wasn't much time for relationship-building, and she didn't make space to clearly communicate how she intended to show up in schools or what she expected from the leaders she now managed.

During the second day of Summer Institute, Jasmine walked into one of her schools and immediately felt frustrated. In her mind, it was obvious: Every member of the school's leadership team should have been standing, actively monitoring, and coaching participants in the training sessions, even if they weren't the ones facilitating. That was her expectation. But it was an expectation she had never actually said out loud.

Instead, she walked into a room where only one leader was up front, facilitating. The rest of the leadership team sat quietly at the back of the room on their laptops, disconnected from the training. No one appeared to be owning the room or actively supporting the teachers in front of them.

Rather than pausing to clarify expectations or asking questions to understand what was going on, Jasmine defaulted to authority. "I need you and your leaders to stand up right now and monitor the impact of this training," she said firmly to the principal. "Make sure everyone is learning what they're supposed to be learning."

The principal responded with hesitation. "We're getting ready for our 'Apply What We Learned' time. My team needs this work time right now."

"I don't care," Jasmine replied. "You need to get up and make sure the current session goes well."

Reluctantly, the team stood and walked around the room. But Jasmine could tell they weren't really engaged, and she was certain that as soon as she left, they'd go right back to what they were doing before. The moment passed, but the damage didn't.

Not only did the training fall flat, but her relationship with the principal was deeply affected. Trust eroded. Over the following months, Jasmine made several attempts to repair the dynamic, but they never fully recovered. The foundation hadn't been laid, and the cracks from that summer moment ran deep. By the end of the year, the principal was no longer on the team.

Looking back, Jasmine realized what went wrong: When expectations go unspoken, and power is used in place of partnership, accountability doesn't stick. And in this case, it came at the cost of both impact and relationship.

Jasmine's story shows what happens when we move too quickly—when we skip the why, skip grounding our actions in values, and skip the conversations that make expectations stick. The result isn't just a missed opportunity for impact; it's a breakdown in trust that's hard to recover from.

OPERATIONALIZING VALUES: FROM WORDS TO DAILY PRACTICE

Once you've named and defined your values and behaviors, don't stop at documentation; bring them to life. Make them part of the daily fabric of your organization: part of hiring, onboarding, evaluations, and team rituals.

Most organizations don't do this.

Brené Brown puts it this way: "Only about 10 percent of organizations have operationalized their values into teachable and observable behaviors that are used to train their employees and hold people accountable. Ten percent. If you're not going to take the time to translate values from ideals to behaviors—if you're not going to teach people the skills they need to show up in a way that's aligned with those values and then create a culture in which you hold one another accountable for staying aligned with the values—it's better not to profess any values at all. They become a joke. A cat poster. Total BS."

High-performing organizations integrate their values into ongoing practices. The best way to do that is by showing people what it looks like in action, every day, in real work.

In my school, we made sure those values weren't just referenced occasionally; they were lived daily. We revisited them in one-to-one check-ins, leadership meetings, and full staff gatherings. They were embedded into our materials: agendas, newsletters, our website, and print collateral. We created space for core value shout-outs during staff meetings, led by staff, not just leadership. Teachers nominated students for exemplifying values, and peers were encouraged to recognize one another, too.

Those values showed up on our walls and in our words—and more importantly, in our actions. I also built in formal reflection points during the year for our leadership team to assess how well we were living those values and report back on patterns and areas for recommitment. By the end of the year, everyone—staff, students, and families—could name them and describe what they looked like in practice.

BUILDING SYSTEMS THAT SUSTAIN VALUES

To embed values into daily operations, we have to do more than name them; we have to build systems that bring them to life. Here's how:

First, build in regular reflection and accountability. As a leadership team, make space during your weekly or biweekly check-ins to reflect on how well you're upholding your values. Talk openly about where you've fallen short and what you'll do differently. This shouldn't just be top-down; create opportunities for your staff to reflect regularly as well.

Second, celebrate values in action. In one of my organizations, we reinforced our values weekly through core value awards. Staff members would recognize their colleagues for embodying specific values, using the actual value language and describing the behavior they saw. That process did two important things: It kept the values alive as part of our culture, and it made it clear that upholding them wasn't just the job of leadership; it was everyone's job.

Finally, leaders have to go first. Modeling the values isn't optional—it's essential. That includes being honest about where you've missed the mark and creating team-wide spaces to reflect on how you're showing up. As a leadership team, we regularly shared where we were upholding the values and where we needed to do better. The more transparent we were, the more permission we gave others to do the same.

These aren't just "nice to haves." They're the foundation for building a values-driven culture that lasts.

WHEN VALUES MEET REALITY: PLANNING FOR IMPERFECTION

Here's the reality: Everyone will fall short of living the values perfectly. You will. Your team will. And that's okay. That's not a failure of the system—it's human nature. Being perfect, while impossible anyway, isn't the point.

The question isn't whether people will miss the mark. The question is: What happens when they do? High-performing organizations don't expect perfection. They expect commitment to getting back on track.

Build this into your values work from the start and continue it throughout. Create safe spaces for people to acknowledge when they've fallen short, recommit to the values, and learn from the experience. Model this yourself by publicly acknowledging when you miss the mark and how you plan to bounce back. When you normalize the recovery process, you remove the shame that keeps people stuck and create a culture of genuine growth rather than performance theater.

WHY THIS FOUNDATION MATTERS

Most organizations don't have a true values system. They may list values on a wall or a website, but those values are often loosely defined—or never translated into action. Tools and systems matter, but they only work when they're anchored in values. You can't spreadsheet your way into trust or checklist your way into culture.

If you study the most successful organizations, one thing stands out: They relentlessly clarify, reinforce, and uphold their values. They don't just state them; they live them. Their values are operationalized through hiring, development, recognition, and accountability. They include clear operating principles, not just abstract ideas.

The strongest accountability systems are led by people who know how to bring purpose into every conversation. As you saw in Jasmine's story, values that remain unspoken can quietly erode trust, but values that are activated through daily leadership can shift an entire culture.

And once those values are clear and embedded, the next step is ensuring everyone knows what's expected—and what support and accountability look like in practice. That's how you build a culture where people don't just know the values, they live them. And when that happens, results follow.

TOOL KIT: PRACTICAL WAYS TO EMBED VALUES INTO DAILY OPERATIONS

Now let's get even more practical. Here's a set of specific, daily strategies to help you embed values into the way your team operates—consistently and clearly.

Five Ways to Build in Regular Reflection and Accountability

1. **Start each leadership meeting** with a five-minute values check-in where each person shares one example of living the values that week.

2. **Add a "values alignment" section** to your meeting agendas to prompt regular discussion.
3. **Use anonymous staff pulse surveys** once a month asking how well the organization is living up to its values.
4. **Incorporate values-based reflection questions** into quarterly staff check-ins.
5. **Create reflective journals or digital prompts** where team members document values wins or misses weekly.

Five Ways to Celebrate Values in Action

1. **Launch a weekly "Values Shout-Out"** in team meetings or newsletters where anyone can highlight a colleague's values-driven action.
2. **Create a physical or digital "Values Wall"** where staff post sticky notes or comments recognizing others.
3. **Include a values spotlight** in monthly all-staff meetings where a story is shared illustrating values in action.
4. **Reward team members quarterly** with a values-based award (small gift or public recognition).
5. **Highlight one value each month** and collect stories or examples across the team to share publicly.

Five Ways to Lead by Example

1. **Set up regular leadership reflection sessions** to name where values were upheld or missed that week.
2. **Publicly acknowledge when you fall short** of a value and share what you'll do differently.
3. **Use your one-to-ones with team members** to talk openly about how you're personally working on certain values.
4. **Share personal stories or experiences** during team meetings where the values challenged or guided your decisions.
5. **Include a values review section** in leadership performance evaluations to create accountability.

CHAPTER 4

EXPECTATIONS CLEAR

"Every system is perfectly designed
to get the results it gets."
—PAUL BATALDEN

Now that your values are clear and embedded into daily practice, you need the next piece of the VERB framework: crystal-clear expectations. Values tell you why something matters. Expectations tell you exactly what needs to happen.

One of the biggest pitfalls I see in leadership is the assumption that simply stating expectations is enough. Leaders often assume that because they've communicated a rule, everyone will follow it. They hope that since people are professionals, they'll hold themselves accountable. But nothing could be further from the truth.

What's more, in addition to stating what needs to be done, teams need clarity about how to do it, what success looks like, and what happens when those expectations aren't met. Without this full picture, teams are left guessing—and guesswork erodes trust, consistency, and results.

Sure, some people will naturally comply, but many won't—not because they're bad employees, but because accountability requires structure, follow-through, and reinforcement.

THE MISSING PIECE: WHAT HAPPENS WHEN EXPECTATIONS AREN'T MET?

Most leaders do set expectations; they have policies about deliverables, deadlines, and attendance. They tell their teams when lesson plans need to be submitted, when reports are due, and what time they are expected to arrive at work. But where they fall short is in planning for what happens when people don't meet those expectations.

Let's take being late as an example.

How many times is it acceptable for someone to be late in your organization or meetings? Twice? Seven times? What if someone is late every single day? At what point do you draw the line? The problem in most organizations is that there is no clear answer to these questions.

Leaders must define not only the expectation but also the consequence of not meeting it. If being late is unacceptable, what happens after the first, second, or fifth offense? Is it a conversation? A written warning? A formal performance improvement plan? What happens next if it continues?

Most leaders don't have an answer to these questions until they're forced to deal with it. And when they make on-the-spot decisions, they end up inconsistent—treating one person one way and another person differently, which opens them up to complaints, confusion, and even legal risk.

BUILDING SYSTEMS THAT MAKE SUCCESS INEVITABLE

Let's take a school environment as an example. Say the expectation is that plans are due every Thursday by 3:00 p.m. That's clear. But then what? High-performing teams don't stop at the ask. They build systems to make sure the ask sticks:

1. THEY PLAN PROACTIVELY

- Who sends reminders?
- Who checks submissions?
- Why does it matter? Teachers need to know this isn't about compliance; it's about instructional quality.

2. THEY DEFINE THE CONSEQUENCE

- What happens if plans are not submitted? What's the follow-up plan?
- Is it a conversation, a reflection form, or something else?
- When and how does it escalate?

When you map all this out in advance, you reduce stress and boost fairness. Teams know what to expect.

Remember that "Strong Start" story from Chapter 1? That school achieved 80 percent proficiency in classroom routines within the first two weeks because we didn't just tell teachers what we expected; we showed them exactly what success looked like through detailed rubrics, practiced it together during summer training, and created daily systems to track and celebrate progress. We made success so clear, teachers would have had to *try* to get it wrong.

That's the power of systematic clarity.

THE SIX ESSENTIAL COMPONENTS
OF CLEAR EXPECTATIONS

Every accountability system should include:

- **What** needs to be done and **when** and **why** it matters
- **How success is defined** and will be measured
- **Who is responsible** for monitoring it
- **How progress** will be tracked
- **What happens** when expectations aren't met
- **How success** is recognized

Clarity reduces anxiety and drives accountability. People want to know where they stand. As Brené Brown wisely notes, "Clear is kind." When expectations are vague or inconsistently applied, ambiguity sets in—and with it comes stress, confusion, and frustration.

When clarity is paired with consistency, employees are far more likely to hold themselves accountable. High performers remain engaged because they recognize that the standards are applied fairly and that their efforts are acknowledged. Meanwhile, team members who are struggling aren't left guessing; they're given specific steps and support to improve rather than being left in limbo.

ACCOUNTABILITY LESSONS FROM UNEXPECTED PLACES

When I talk to education leaders about accountability, they often picture checklists, evaluations, or awkward conversations with staff. But let me tell you, some of the best examples of accountability I've ever seen didn't come from schools. They came from real estate, my second passion.

THE LANDLORD WHO GETS IT RIGHT

Let's start with Matt. We'll call him a "landlord," but he operates more like an accountability ninja. Matt runs a portfolio of single-family rentals, and while his units are nice, his secret weapon isn't fancy appliances or luxury vinyl plank flooring. It's his quarterly inspection system.

"I believe in the power of presence," he told me once. "People behave differently when they know they're being held accountable."

Every three months, Matt or someone from his team stops by each property to change the air filter. Sounds minor, right? But it's a brilliant move. While they're there, they do a quick walk-through, check for any maintenance issues, and—without ever raising their voice or wagging a finger—they remind tenants that someone is paying attention.

The accountability is built into the structure. It's quiet, consistent, and incredibly effective. Tenants take better care of the space. Mechanical systems last longer. And small issues are caught before they turn into expensive problems. Matt doesn't just "expect" care; he inspects for it. And that simple act sets the tone.

THE STAGER WHO CHANGED MY BEHAVIOR

I recently worked with two different home staging companies while prepping two different investment properties for sale. Both got the job done. But one taught me a master class in how clarity shifts behavior.

The first stager was...fine. We picked a date, they brought in the furniture, and they staged the property. It was understood—though never explicitly said—that no further renovations should happen once the furniture was in. But "understood" doesn't mean "clear."

So what happened? Well, our contractors came back for a few

touch-ups. Nothing major, just a ceiling scuff here, a missed spot of trim there. We didn't even think to warn them to be careful. It was all very casual.

Now compare that to stager number two.

Before we even scheduled a date, she made it clear—in bold letters on her contract—that if any of her furniture was damaged, we'd pay a replacement fee. And it wasn't small. She also followed up with an email as we got closer to the install date: "Just a reminder, no contractors in the house after staging. I've had rugs ruined and coffee tables scuffed."

Let me tell you, I was on my team like a hawk. I sent texts, left voicemails, reminded the crew daily: Don't touch the staging furniture. Don't breathe too hard near the staging furniture. Why? Because the expectation was clear, the consequences were real, and the communication was repeated.

The difference? I didn't just know the expectation; I believed it mattered. And I changed my behavior because of it.

Both examples—Matt the landlord and the crystal-clear stager—highlight one powerful truth: **Accountability isn't about being harsh. It's about being clear, consistent, and present.**

Whether it's a tenant who takes better care of their apartment or a real estate investor who tiptoes around staged furniture like it's the Louvre, people rise (or fall) to the level of what's expected—and what's checked.

As educators, we can learn from this. Presence matters. Follow-up matters. And clarity? That might just be the most underestimated accountability lever of all.

THE POWER OF PUBLIC PRAISE AND PRIVATE ACCOUNTABILITY

One of the best strategies for reinforcing clarity in accountability is praise. Public celebration of those who frequently meet or exceed expectations is a great reminder to all of what's expected.

If your team sees that those who do the work are recognized, celebrated, and valued, it creates a powerful motivator for everyone else.

People naturally want to be included when they see others being recognized. If there's a weekly recognition of high performers and someone's name is never mentioned, they'll start to feel the weight of their own inaction.

But here's the key: Praise publicly; address problems privately. When someone isn't meeting expectations, that conversation happens one-on-one, with clarity, support, and a plan for improvement. This approach builds trust while maintaining standards.

MAKING EXPECTATIONS STICK

The best people on your team crave clarity. They want to know the goal, how to hit it, and that everyone's playing by the same rules. When that happens, energy rises. Trust builds. Results follow.

Clear expectations don't have to be rigid; they can be a powerful lever that creates momentum. They give people the confidence to act, the direction to improve, and the motivation to keep going. When everyone knows what's expected, how to get there, and that follow-through is real, you unlock a culture where people feel seen, supported, and proud of what they're building together.

This is what great teams are made of.

TOOL KIT: BUILD YOUR CLARITY-DRIVEN ACCOUNTABILITY SYSTEM

Clarity doesn't happen by accident. It's designed, communicated, reinforced, and revisited. To make expectations unmissable—and accountability inevitable—try these actionable steps to embed the learning from this chapter into your daily leadership practice.

Step 1: Pick One High-Stakes Expectation

Think of one critical expectation that, if consistently met, would move the needle for your team or organization. It could be:

- Submitting lesson plans on time
- Arriving to morning meetings prepared
- Turning in student data trackers weekly
- Starting class on time with a clear Do Now

Start small. One expectation. One system.

Step 2: Define What Success Looks Like

Now, get specific. Use this prompt: *If someone walked into a room and saw this expectation being met, what would they actually see or hear?*

Write out the exact behaviors—for both the staff member and students, if applicable. Think in rubrics, not vibes.

Step 3: Make It Public and Practice It

Communicate the expectation to your team—clearly. Show them the rubric, talk through it, and if it's operational (like a routine), practice it together. Normalize the expectation before it ever becomes a compliance issue.

Step 4: Create an Observation and Feedback Plan

Who is responsible for checking this?

- How often?
- What tool will they use?
- How will they share progress?

You don't need a fancy tracker, just consistency and visibility. Decide how progress will be shared and celebrated.

Step 5: Define What Happens If It's Not Met

Don't wait until something goes off the rails to decide what the consequence is. Outline a progression:

1. **First miss** = friendly reminder or check-in
2. **Second** = note in tracker or reflection form
3. **Third** = follow-up conversation with next steps

Consistency here is what builds trust—not harshness.

Step 6: Celebrate Those Who Get It Right

Choose one small but visible way to recognize progress:

- A shout-out in a huddle
- A leaderboard update
- A personal thank-you
- A silly certificate or emoji sticker—make it yours

Accountability works better when it feels like belonging, not punishment.

Final Challenge:

Make it so clear they'd have to _try_ to get it wrong.

You've got the tools. Now, pick the one expectation you'll clarify this week, and commit to reinforcing it for the next two.

Let clarity do its job. You'll be amazed at what changes.

CHAPTER 5

REAL PROGRESS

---

*"The scoreboard doesn't lie. You
are getting the results your
system is designed to produce."*
—CHRIS MCCHESNEY, *THE 4
DISCIPLINES OF EXECUTION*

You've established your values. You've set crystal-clear expectations. Now comes the moment of truth: follow-through. This is where the VERB framework either comes alive or falls apart. Because without Real Progress—without consistent tracking, feedback, and course-correction—even the best values and clearest expectations become meaningless.

Real Progress is about more than checking boxes or catching mistakes. It's about creating a rhythm of accountability that supports people, celebrates wins, and ensures that what matters most actually happens. But here's what most leaders miss: Effective follow-through isn't about authority; it's about purpose.

Let me show you what I mean.

LEADING WITH PURPOSE, NOT POWER

Darien thought he was being efficient. He had a full plate, a looming deadline, and a plan that made sense—on paper. But what he hadn't yet learned was this: Accountability isn't about enforcing plans. It's about protecting purpose.

His story reveals the difference between holding the line and building alignment—and why follow-through that centers values, not just tasks, is the real lever for sustainable success.

When Malik, a nonprofit leadership coach, began working with Eastpoint Charter Schools, he was assigned to support a first-year principal named Darien. Darien had all the makings of a strong leader—he was smart, driven, and deeply committed to his students—but he was still learning how to lead adults in a way that connected to values, not just tasks.

One afternoon, as Malik walked through the hallway toward Darien's office for their scheduled coaching session, he overheard a tense exchange just outside the door. A teacher asked, "Hey, would it be okay if we rescheduled our data meeting? Something's come up."

Darien responded, "I really need this to happen right now. I have to submit a coaching video today. This is the only time I have. Can we please just stick to the plan?"

The teacher nodded, clearly disappointed, and walked away.

A few seconds later, Malik stepped into the office. Darien, still flustered, gestured toward the hallway. "Did you hear that? I told her we couldn't reschedule. I've got to get this video submitted today. This was my one window."

Malik nodded. "I heard. Can I ask, what was the goal of the data meeting with her?"

Darien answered quickly, "To review her student work, identify next steps, and coach her on how to adjust instruction. That's what we always do."

"And what was her goal in that moment?"

Darien paused. "I guess...to get some flexibility. Something personal probably came up."

Malik nodded again. "You were trying to protect the system. I get that. But what you missed was an opportunity to protect the *why* behind it. You had a moment to connect her to the purpose of that meeting, not just hold her to the schedule."

Darien sat back. "Yeah...I made it about the video, not the learning. Not the bigger picture."

Malik added, "And in that moment, you were leading with authority, not purpose. You held the line, but you didn't build alignment. Accountability rooted in power rarely builds trust."

Then he said, "Let's replay it."

Darien looked puzzled. "Replay it?"

"Yeah," Malik said. "Let's walk through that moment again, this time with your values in the lead. What do you wish you'd said?"

Darien paused, then tried, "Something like, 'I understand something came up, and I want to be supportive. At the same time, these data meetings are core to our work. This is where we make sure our kids are getting what they need. Can we figure out a way to honor both?'"

Malik smiled. "That right there—that's leadership. That's alignment to your *why*. You acknowledged her, reinforced purpose, and invited her into a solution. And you set the tone for accountability rooted in values, not deadlines."

From that moment forward, Darien began to shift. He practiced leading with purpose first, especially under pressure. With Malik's coaching, he started to show up differently—offering clarity without control, and holding high expectations without losing connection.

What started as a hallway misstep became a breakthrough. Darien learned that real accountability isn't about guarding the plan—it's about guarding the purpose. And purpose always out-performs power.

WHY MOST LEADERS FAIL AT FOLLOW-THROUGH

One of the biggest reasons leaders fail to get results is simple: They don't follow up. They assume that once they set an expectation, their team will execute. They rely on hope as a strategy—and it doesn't work.

There are three main reasons this happens:

First, leaders assume positive intent. They believe their people will do what they're supposed to because they're professionals. While positive intent is admirable, it's not a management strategy.

Second, leaders often feel they don't have time to check in and inspect what they expect. They get caught up in meetings, emails, and administrative tasks that don't move the needle, leaving accountability on the back burner.

Finally, many leaders confuse follow-up with micromanagement—and because they don't want to seem like they're hovering, they don't check in at all.

But here's the truth: Effective leaders understand that follow-up isn't micromanagement; it's leadership. It's about supporting your team to ensure they succeed.

BUILDING A SYSTEM FOR REAL PROGRESS

Real Progress requires four key components that work together as a system:

1. STRUCTURED CHECK-INS: MAKE FOLLOW-UP EXPECTED, NOT INTRUSIVE

The first step to effective follow-up happens before you even roll out an initiative or set an expectation. You must clearly communicate how follow-up will happen, why it matters, and what it will look like in action. If people know in advance that their progress will be checked—not as a "gotcha" but as a form of support—they'll be far more likely to engage with the process.

Example: Let's take professional development in an organization. The goal is for employees to learn a skill and implement it effectively. But what often happens? They attend the PD, and then nothing changes. Why? Because no one follows up.

Instead, announce up front: "After this training, I'll be checking in with each of you in two weeks to see how implementation is going and what support you need. Then we'll have a team debrief in four weeks to share what's working and troubleshoot challenges together." This isn't micromanaging; it's creating a structure for success.

2. CONSISTENT PRESENCE: IF YOU SAY YOU'LL FOLLOW UP, FOLLOW UP

Leaders often set expectations but fail to prioritize checking in. If you tell your team you'll be in classrooms to observe a new teaching strategy—or you'll be reviewing sales calls, reports, or project updates—you need to show up. If you don't, people will quickly learn that follow-up isn't serious, and they'll stop taking expectations seriously.

The biggest challenge here is time management. Leaders need to be intentional about blocking time on their calendar for follow-ups and ensuring that checking progress is a nonnegotiable part of their leadership routine.

Pro Tip: Treat follow-up appointments like client meetings.

They're nonnegotiable unless there's a true emergency. Your team's progress is just as important as any external commitment.

3. DATA-DRIVEN TRACKING: YOU CAN'T MANAGE WHAT YOU DON'T MEASURE

If you're not measuring it, you're only guessing. Say you set an expectation that 80 percent of your team should be implementing a new strategy within a month, how will you know it's actually happening?

Many leaders assume they have a good sense of how things are going, but assumptions are often wrong. I once asked a new school leader what percentage of teachers were implementing a new instructional strategy. She guessed about 60 percent. When she checked, it was actually 20 percent. Without data, she would have continued believing things were going well when, in reality, only a fraction of her team had followed through.

A simple tracker can change everything. Whether it's a shared spreadsheet, a project management tool, or a structured progress report, having a system to measure execution removes ambiguity and ensures that both leaders and employees know where they stand.

Example Tracker Elements:

- Team member name
- Implementation goal
- Current status (not started/in progress/proficient)
- Date of last check-in
- Support needed
- Next steps

4. RESPONSIVE SUPPORT: PLAN FOR THE MISS

Not everyone will meet expectations the first time. That's normal. But the real question is: What do you do about it?

When someone falls short, leaders need to be ready to:

- **Identify why** they aren't meeting expectations (lack of clarity? lack of skill? lack of motivation?)
- **Provide additional support** (coaching, feedback, training)
- **Decide on next steps** if performance doesn't improve

Having a clear system for addressing gaps prevents last-minute decision-making and ensures fairness and consistency. Without this, follow-up becomes inconsistent, and employees see accountability as arbitrary rather than structured and supportive.

THE POWER OF CELEBRATING PROGRESS

Tracking progress isn't just about catching what's wrong; it's also about recognizing what's right. Data should be used not only to course-correct but to celebrate wins.

When teams see their growth measured and acknowledged, they feel more motivated to sustain high performance. If you have a tracker that shows progress toward a goal, use it as an opportunity to highlight those who are excelling. Public recognition can be a powerful motivator for everyone else to level up their performance.

Example: "I want to shout out Maria, James, and Sandra. All three have been implementing our new engagement strategies consistently for two weeks straight, and their students are responding incredibly well. Let's hear from them about what's working."

This does two things: It rewards the behavior you want to see more of, and it gives struggling team members concrete examples of success to learn from.

MAKING IT SUSTAINABLE: YOUR FOLLOW-THROUGH RHYTHM

Real Progress isn't about perfection; it's about consistency. Here's how to build a sustainable rhythm:

Weekly: Quick check-ins with key team members or departments

Biweekly: Deeper dives into progress data and individual support needs

Monthly: Team-wide progress reviews and celebration of wins

Quarterly: Systems evaluation—what's working, what needs adjustment?

The key is finding a rhythm that works for your team and sticking to it. Consistency builds trust. Sporadic follow-up builds frustration.

FROM PROGRESS TO OWNERSHIP

Real Progress sets the stage for the final piece of the VERB Framework: Buy-In and Ownership. When people see that you're genuinely tracking progress to support their success—not to catch their failures—they start to own the process themselves. They begin self-correcting, supporting colleagues, and pushing themselves because they believe in what they're building.

That's when accountability transforms from something you do *to* your team into something they do *with* you. And that's where sustainable, long-term success lives.

TOOL KIT: BUILDING YOUR REAL PROGRESS SYSTEM

Ready to move from hoping people follow through to knowing they will? Use this step-by-step guide to build a system that supports success and drives results.

Step 1: Choose Your Tracking Method

Pick one tool that you'll actually use consistently:

- **Simple spreadsheet** with team member names, goals, and status updates
- **Project management tool** like Asana, Monday, or Trello
- **Shared document** with progress indicators and next steps
- **Weekly email template** that standardizes check-ins

The best system is the one you'll actually maintain.

Step 2: Design Your Check-In Rhythm

Block time on your calendar for:

- **Daily** (five minutes): Reviewing your tracker and identifying who needs support
- **Weekly** (thirty minutes): Checking in with three to five team members individually
- **Biweekly** (sixty minutes): Deep diving into progress data and support planning
- **Monthly** (ninety minutes): Leading a team progress meeting with celebration and troubleshooting

Step 3: Create Your Response Playbook

Before someone gets off track, decide:

If someone misses once:

- Friendly check-in: "How's implementation going? What support do you need?"

If someone misses twice:

- Coaching conversation: "I've noticed X. Let's problem-solve together."

If it's a pattern:

- Create a formal support plan with specific steps and timeline.

Step 4: Build In Celebration

Plan how you'll recognize progress:

- Weekly team meeting shout-outs
- Monthly progress newsletters
- Quarterly success stories
- Year-end achievement recognition

Step 5: Test and Adjust

Start with one initiative or expectation. Use your system for thirty days, then evaluate:

- What's working well?
- Where are you getting stuck?
- What needs to be simplified?

- How is your team responding?

Adjust based on what you learn, then expand to other areas.

Your Real Progress Challenge

Pick one current expectation that isn't being met consistently. Apply this system for the next month:

1. Set up your tracker.
2. Communicate your follow-up plan to your team.
3. Block time for consistent check-ins.
4. Celebrate progress along the way.

Remember: The goal isn't perfection; it's progress. And progress, tracked and supported consistently, always leads to results.

CHAPTER 6

BUY-IN AND OWNERSHIP

*"When accountability is
present, people keep their
eyes on a very clear prize."*
—PATRICK LENCIONI

You've established your values, set clear expectations, and built systems for tracking real progress. Now comes the final piece of the VERB framework, and arguably the most important one: Buy-In and Ownership.

This is where accountability transforms from something you manage to something your team drives. When people truly own the work, they don't need you to check on them constantly. They check on themselves. They support each other. They push themselves because they believe in what they're building.

But here's what most leaders get wrong: They try to create buy-in after they've already made all the decisions. They present a finished plan and then wonder why people aren't excited about it.

If you want your team to own the work, they have to help build it. Buy-in doesn't happen after the plan; it happens during it. One of the most overlooked truths about leadership is this: People support what they help create.

CREATING LEADERSHIP WHERE IT DIDN'T EXIST

At my school, I learned that buy-in wasn't just about getting people to agree; it was about making people feel seen, valued, and involved. And it didn't always take a huge effort. In fact, some of the smallest moves made the biggest difference.

One of the most powerful ways I built buy-in was by developing leadership at every level. I created leadership opportunities that didn't previously exist, because I wasn't just trying to lead a strong school. I was trying to build a bench that could sustain the work long after I was gone.

That meant investing heavily in my secondary leadership team—assistant principals, deans, and operations leads—and giving them real ownership over critical aspects of our school. But it didn't stop there. I also created instructional teacher leader roles. Some of these were standard positions, like house leaders, but others were brand-new roles I designed to tap into the talent on our team.

These roles came with a small stipend, sure. But what mattered most was that they came with big responsibility, and real ownership. These teacher leaders weren't just mouthpieces to carry a message. We brought them in during the ideation phase. They brainstormed with us, poked holes in half-baked plans, and helped us make those plans stronger. They gave feedback on how to message changes, how to anticipate pushback, and how to position new work in a way that would land well with the broader staff.

Why? Because they had influence. And sometimes, peer influence is even more powerful than top-down authority. These teachers became our internal champions; not because we asked them to, but because they believed in what they helped shape.

FROM IDEA TO OWNERSHIP

There's a huge difference between being informed and being invited. When people are informed, they get the memo. When they're invited, they become part of the build. We invited our teacher leaders to help us shape the work, and it paid off. Even when someone wasn't fully aligned with the final version, the fact that they were part of the process made them more willing to support the plan. They could say, "We built this," not just, "Leadership told us to."

When we launched new initiatives, I gave our teacher leaders full ownership, from designing the rollout to managing the implementation to tracking progress and reporting back. I leaned heavily into the concept of "extreme ownership" (shout-out to Jocko Willink and Leif Babin's book by the same name). If a teacher leader owned something, they owned all of it. And we trained them accordingly. The bar was high, but so was the trust.

THE POWER OF WORKING GROUPS: SMALL TEAMS, BIG IMPACT

One of the most effective strategies I used for building buy-in was forming small, nimble working groups to tackle specific problems. These weren't formal committees. Just a few trusted voices, a clear problem, and a chance to shape the solution.

Here's an example: In our founding year, our sixth-grade math scores were second to last in the network. That was unacceptable to me. So I pulled two teachers from the sixth-grade team and said, "Let's go observe one of the best math teachers in the network and see what we can learn."

What they didn't know was that this wasn't just about sixth grade. I was planning to let them influence math instruction across the entire school.

After observing two full lessons and spending hours debriefing, we created a new instructional approach: a "key chain" model for math. Those two teachers led everything: the messaging, the rollout, the training of other math teachers. I supported them, but I didn't own it. They did.

And it worked. Our math scores skyrocketed, from second-to-last to consistently in the top three across the network. Not because of a mandate, but because of ownership.

The beauty of working groups is that they're small enough to move quickly but influential enough to create change. When you hand ownership to a small team of trusted people, they become your internal change agents. They understand the work deeply because they helped create it, and they can advocate for it authentically because they believe in it.

MODELING TRUST THROUGH STRATEGIC RISK-TAKING

Buy-in isn't always loud. Sometimes it looks like trust. One of the most brilliant examples I've seen came from a colleague at one of the highest-performing charter networks in Missouri—and arguably in the country.

Hannah Lofthus leads with surgical precision and extraordinary intentionality. At one point, a teacher proposed a major shift in school culture—a classic "pendulum swing" idea. Hannah was well aware of the pendulum swings happening in high-performing charter networks nationwide. Many of these schools received feedback about their "rigid" structures, and instead of thoughtfully considering what adjustments were needed, they often overcorrected, stripping away valuable structures.

When a teacher suggested a similar shift, Hannah could have easily dismissed it, armed with evidence of past failures. But instead, she chose a different approach: "Let's try it. In one classroom. For a short period. And then let's assess together."

She let the teacher test the idea, but on her terms. Limited scope. Limited timeline. Strategic classroom where they could easily pivot back if needed. And within days, the teacher came back and said, "This isn't going to work."

Now that's how you cultivate buy-in. Not from convincing, but from experiencing. She gave space, held the guardrails, and let the work speak for itself. Her team trusts her deeply because she treats them like collaborators, not compliance officers.

This approach does something powerful: It shows your team that you value their thinking, you're willing to take calculated risks on their ideas, and you trust them to learn from the data. Even when the idea doesn't work, the trust and respect you've built by letting them try it creates deeper buy-in for future decisions.

MANAGE THE NARRATIVE—OR SOMEONE ELSE WILL

If you don't actively shape the culture of your team, someone else will. And spoiler alert: it's rarely the person you want leading the charge. More often, it's the loudest voice in the room, and let's be real, the loudest voice is frequently the most negative, the most resistant, or the one who still misses the mute button on Zoom.

Every team has informal leaders—the people everyone secretly looks to for validation, even if they don't have a fancy title. If you're not steering the ship, these folks will. And let me tell you, their destination might not be anywhere near where you're trying to go.

That's why leadership isn't a one-time mic-drop moment. It's a relentless, and yes sometimes repetitive, drumbeat of expectations, values, and norms. You can't just "set the tone" once and expect everyone to hum along forever; this is not a one-hit-wonder situation. When leaders allow ambiguity, dysfunction creeps in. But when you lead with consistency, you leave no room for the wrong voices to fill the silence.

I learned this the hard way. Early in my leadership journey, I truly believed if I said something once—maybe twice—everyone got it. Hilarious, right? Turns out, humans need to hear something multiple times and in different ways before it sticks. Repetition is not redundant; it's required.

That means weaving your organization's mission, values, and expectations into everyday moments. Use stories, analogies, memes, pop culture—whatever keeps it alive and relatable. And above all, start with the why. People don't buy into rules; they buy into reasons. Help them see what's at stake, why it matters, and what's in it for them.

CELEBRATE MORE THAN YOU CORRECT

Now, let me give you one of the most overlooked—but absolute magic—moves for driving accountability: Celebrate wins more than you correct mistakes.

Here's the thing: nobody (and I mean nobody) wakes up excited to attend the "what you did wrong" meeting. But people do lean in when they see their peers being recognized, praised, and even rewarded for showing up the right way.

Use public praise to spotlight those exceeding expectations. Drop their names in team meetings. Send out an all-staff shout-out. Create a leaderboard if you're feeling spicy. Peer recognition has a funny way of making everyone want a seat at the table.

Just remember, not everyone likes being put on blast, even for good stuff. Learn what feels good for your team: Some love the spotlight; others might melt into the floor. A sticky note, a Slack message, or an actual thank-you card (yes, those still exist) can go a long way.

The point is, what you celebrate gets repeated. And if the only thing people hear from you is what they did wrong, don't be surprised when they stop showing up at all.

When you celebrate publicly and specifically, you do three things:

1. You reinforce the behaviors you want to see more of
2. You give others concrete examples of what success looks like
3. You signal that meeting expectations matters and is noticed

This isn't about participation trophies or false praise. It's about strategically recognizing the behaviors and outcomes that align with your values and move your organization forward.

THE VERB FRAMEWORK IN ACTION

When all four components of the VERB framework work together, something magical happens:

- **Values First** creates the foundation and the "why" behind everything you do.
- **Expectations Clear** removes ambiguity and gives people a concrete target.
- **Real Progress** provides the feedback loop that keeps everyone on track.
- **Buy-In and Ownership** transforms compliance into commitment.

The result? Accountability that doesn't depend on you constantly managing it. Your team starts to self-correct, support each other, and push themselves because they believe in what they're building together.

This is the difference between leading a team and building a culture. Teams can perform well when the leader is present. Cultures perform well because the systems, values, and ownership are embedded in how they operate.

BUILDING SUSTAINABLE SUCCESS

The ultimate goal of the VERB framework isn't just better performance in the short term; it's creating a self-sustaining system where accountability becomes part of your organization's DNA. When you've done this right:

- People hold themselves accountable before you have to
- Team members support and coach each other
- Problems get identified and solved quickly
- Excellence becomes the expectation, not the exception
- Your best people stay because they're part of something they believe in

This is what separates good leaders from great ones. Good leaders can drive results through their own effort and oversight. Great leaders build systems and cultures that drive results even when they're not in the room.

TOOL KIT: BUILDING BUY-IN THAT LASTS

Ready to transform your team from compliant to committed? Use these strategies to create genuine ownership and shared accountability.

Strategy 1: Create Authentic Leadership Opportunities

- **Identify informal influencers** on your team, people others naturally look to for guidance.
- **Design meaningful roles** that come with real responsibility, not just extra tasks.
- **Include them in planning** before decisions are made, not after.
- **Give them ownership** over entire processes, from design to implementation.
- **Support their success** with training, resources, and regular check-ins.

Action Step: This week, identify one person who could take ownership of a current challenge. Meet with them to explore how they might lead the solution.

Strategy 2: Form Strategic Working Groups

- **Keep them small** (three to five people max) for speed and focus.
- **Choose diverse perspectives** to ensure well-rounded solutions.
- **Give clear parameters** about what they can and cannot change.
- **Set specific timelines** with regular check-in points.
- **Let them own the rollout** once the solution is developed.

Action Step: Pick one current problem and form a working group to tackle it. Give them thirty days to develop and present a solution.

Strategy 3: Practice Strategic Risk-Taking

- **Listen to all proposals** with genuine curiosity, even if you disagree.
- **Find low-risk ways** to test new ideas (pilot programs, limited scope).
- **Set clear success metrics** up front so everyone knows how to evaluate results.
- **Debrief together** regardless of whether the idea works or fails.
- **Celebrate the learning** that comes from thoughtful experimentation.

Action Step: The next time someone proposes an idea you're skeptical about, ask yourself: "How could we test this safely?"

Strategy 4: Build Your Celebration System

- **Make recognition specific** by naming exactly what someone did well.
- **Match the recognition style** to what each person appreciates.
- **Celebrate both outcomes and behaviors** that align with your values.
- **Use multiple channels** (meetings, emails, one-on-ones, public boards).
- **Create peer-to-peer recognition** opportunities, not just top-down praise.

Action Step: This week, publicly recognize three people for specific behaviors that exemplify your values.

Strategy 5: Control the Narrative

- **Identify your informal leaders** and invest in relationships with them.
- **Communicate consistently** across multiple channels and formats.
- **Repeat key messages** in different ways until you're tired of saying them.
- **Address resistance directly** rather than hoping it will go away.
- **Share stories** that illustrate your values and expectations in action.

Action Step: List your team's informal leaders. Schedule one-on-one time with each of them this month.

Your Buy-In Challenge

Choose one initiative or expectation that currently feels like a struggle. Apply the ownership approach:

1. **Identify two to three people** who could help shape the solution.
2. **Invite them into the planning** process before making decisions.
3. **Give them real ownership** over part of the implementation.
4. **Support their success** with whatever resources they need.
5. **Celebrate their contributions** publicly and specifically.

Remember: The goal isn't to make everyone happy; it's to make everyone invested. When people help build something, they fight to make it work.

PART 3

MASTERING THE HUMAN SIDE

CHAPTER 7

TOUGH CONVERSATIONS THAT BUILD TRUST

---

*"Daring leaders are never
silent about hard things."*
—Brené Brown

You've built the VERB framework. Your values are clear, expectations are set, you're tracking real progress, and you've created Buy-In and Ownership. But here's the reality: Even with the best systems in place, you'll still need to have tough conversations.

People will miss deadlines. Performance will slip. Attitudes will need adjusting. And when those moments come, how you handle them will determine whether your accountability system strengthens or crumbles.

Welcome to Part 3: Mastering the Human Side of accountability. This is where theory meets reality, where frameworks face feelings, and where your leadership skills get tested most. Because accountability isn't just about systems; it's about people. And people are complicated, emotional, and sometimes resistant to change.

The good news? Tough conversations don't have to kill morale. In fact, when done right, they can actually build trust, clarify expectations, and strengthen your culture. But you have to know how to navigate them skillfully.

THE COST OF AVOIDANCE

Let's be honest, nobody loves tough conversations. In fact, most leaders avoid them like a bad group text: reading the message, feeling guilty, and then pretending it'll magically resolve itself.

The problem is, it never does. That's the thing about accountability: the longer you wait, the bigger the mess. Left unchecked, one person's low performance turns into everyone else's resentment. Suddenly, your team's top performers are wondering why they're carrying the weight—and why you're not doing anything about it.

Here's the truth most leadership books skip: **Avoiding hard conversations is what actually kills morale—not the conversation itself.**

And yet, leaders avoid them for three reasons we've all either experienced or been guilty of:

1. **Fear of damaging relationships:** What if I upset them? What if they quit? What if it's awkward and we both pretend it didn't happen?
2. **Uncertainty about how to say it:** Will I make it worse? What if I freeze up? What if I don't have the right words?
3. **Hoping it'll fix itself:** Maybe they're just having a rough week...or month...or year.

Here's the hard truth: **Avoiding the conversation does more damage than having it.** Poor performance doesn't improve with silence; it multiplies. High performers get frustrated. Culture erodes. And that "small" issue you were hoping would go away? It's running the place now.

THE MINDSET SHIFT: FOUR THINGS LEADERS NEED TO REMEMBER

Before we dive into how to have these conversations, you need to reframe your mindset. Because your mindset, going in? That sets the tone for everything else.

1. CLARITY IS KINDNESS

You're not being harsh. You're being clear. Ambiguity creates anxiety; the more specific you are, the less room there is for drama or misunderstanding. When you leave someone guessing about their performance, you're not being nice; you're being cruel.

2. ACCOUNTABILITY CONVERSATIONS ARE A GIFT

Real talk: Feedback is an investment, not a punishment. If you're too "nice" to be honest, you're robbing someone of their shot to grow. The people who care about doing good work want to know where they stand and how they can improve.

3. YOUR TEAM IS WATCHING

Every time you dodge a hard conversation, you send a message: We tolerate mediocrity here. Your high performers notice. If you don't address issues, you lose the respect of the people who are actually doing the work.

4. TOUGH CONVERSATIONS AREN'T ONE-TIME EVENTS

You don't get to tick the box and move on. Real accountability is built through follow-up, coaching, and making sure change actually happens.

THE GAME CHANGER: PUT THE COGNITIVE LOAD ON YOUR TEAM

Here's where most leaders get accountability conversations wrong: They do all the thinking. They walk into the conversation with a script, read it aloud, and wait for the person across from them to nod awkwardly. Zero ownership.

If you've clearly set expectations and reinforced values through the VERB framework, your team already knows what's expected of them. So flip it. Stop telling; start asking.

INSTEAD OF THIS:

"The expectation was that lesson plans would be submitted by Thursday at 3:00 p.m. You've missed the deadline three times this month. This is unacceptable and needs to stop immediately."

TRY THIS:

- "Can you remind me what our expectation is around lesson plan submission?"
- "How do you think you've been doing with meeting that expectation?"
- "What impact do you think this has on our team and our students?"
- "What do you think needs to happen next?"

When people have to say it out loud, they own it. And real talk? People are often harsher on themselves than we are. The magic happens when the person drives the accountability conversation instead of being dragged through it.

THE POWER OF COCREATING SOLUTIONS

Even when creating support plans, involve them in the process. Don't hand them a twelve-step prescriptive plan. Ask them to draft the plan. They know their gaps. They know what it'll take. And when they build it, they're way more likely to follow through.

Example dialogue: *"Based on what we've discussed, what kind of support do you think would be most helpful? What would a plan look like that sets you up for success? Draft something and let's meet again tomorrow to review it together."*

This approach does three powerful things:

1. It creates ownership instead of compliance.
2. It respects their intelligence and professionalism.
3. It makes them a partner in the solution, not a victim of consequences.

THE TIMELINE THAT PREVENTS CRISIS MANAGEMENT

The biggest mistake leaders make is waiting too long to have the tough conversation. By that point, the damage is done, and so is your credibility.

You need a clear system and timeline for when conversations need to happen. Otherwise, you'll always default to avoiding them.

Every organization should know:

- How long is too long to tolerate underperformance?
- When should the first conversation happen?
- At what point does formal support kick in?

- What's the timeline before it's clear this isn't a fit?

EXAMPLE TIMELINE FROM MY WORLD:

- **By October:** Struggling employees identified and support plans started
- **By November:** Progress monitored with regular coaching and check-ins
- **By December:** Decisions made—improvement or next steps
- **And, yes:** We planned ahead for potential turnover, so we weren't caught scrambling

This level of intentionality ensures that leaders don't delay hard conversations out of fear or uncertainty. Define the timeline up front, or risk being that leader everyone is waiting on to act.

THE CONVERSATION FRAMEWORK: A STEP-BY-STEP APPROACH

When it's time to have the conversation, here's a framework that works:

1. SET THE STAGE (THIRTY SECONDS)

"I want to talk with you about [specific situation]. This isn't about punishment; it's about making sure you have what you need to be successful here."

2. ESTABLISH THE FACTS (TWO TO THREE MINUTES)

"Can you walk me through what happened with [specific example]?" Let them talk first. Listen. Ask clarifying questions.

3. CONNECT TO IMPACT (TWO TO THREE MINUTES)

"Help me understand—what impact do you think this had on [the team/students/project]?" "How do you think this aligns with our values around [specific value]?"

4. CO-CREATE THE SOLUTION (FIVE TO TEN MINUTES)

"What do you think needs to change?" "What kind of support would be most helpful?" "What would success look like moving forward?"

5. CONFIRM NEXT STEPS (TWO MINUTES)

"So just to make sure we're on the same page, you're going to [specific action] by [specific date], and I'm going to [specific support]. Does that sound right?"

6. SCHEDULE FOLLOW-UP

"Let's check in again on [specific date] to see how things are going."

THE REAL WORK IS IN THE FOLLOW-THROUGH

Here's the thing no one tells you: The conversation is just the starting point. What happens next? That's where leadership shows up.

- **Check back in:** Don't assume progress. Schedule the follow-up and keep it.
- **Reinforce expectations:** If things slip again, address it right away.
- **Balance correction with recognition:** If the only time people hear from you is when something's wrong, don't be surprised when they stop listening.

Remember, this isn't about being liked. It's about being respected. The best leaders don't just say the hard thing; they follow through on it. And that's what earns trust.

WHEN CONVERSATIONS DON'T WORK

Sometimes, despite your best efforts, the conversations don't lead to change. That's when you need to be prepared for the next level of intervention:

- **Formal performance improvement plans** with specific metrics and timelines
- **Increased supervision and support** with daily or weekly check-ins
- **Role adjustments** that better match their strengths and the organization's needs
- **Transition planning** when it becomes clear the fit isn't right

The key is having these escalation steps planned in advance, not scrambling to figure them out when you're frustrated and out of options.

BUILDING A CULTURE WHERE TOUGH CONVERSATIONS FEEL NORMAL

The ultimate goal isn't to become better at having difficult conversations; it's to build a culture where feedback is so normal that conversations rarely feel difficult. When you've implemented the VERB framework consistently, when expectations are clear and progress is tracked regularly, most issues get addressed before they become problems.

In high-accountability cultures:

- People expect feedback and ask for it regularly.
- Small course corrections happen in real time.
- The big, scary conversations become rare.
- When tough conversations do happen, they feel supportive rather than punitive.

But even with the best conversation skills and clearest expectations, you'll still encounter pushback. Some people will resist change, make excuses, or actively challenge your leadership. When that happens, you need to handle resistance like a pro—and that requires a different set of skills entirely.

TOOL KIT: YOUR STEP-BY-STEP GUIDE

Ready to transform how you handle tough conversations? Use these tools to make difficult discussions productive and relationship-building.

Preconversation Checklist

Before scheduling any accountability conversation, ask yourself:

☐ **Have I been clear about expectations?** (Don't have the conversation if the answer is no. Get clear first.)

☐ **Do I have specific examples?** (Vague feedback creates defensiveness.)

☐ **What's my desired outcome?** (Behavior change, improved performance, or transition planning?)

☐ **Am I in the right mindset?** (Frustrated? Cool down first. Caring and firm? Perfect.)

☐ **Have I scheduled enough time?** (These conversations can't be rushed.)

The CLEAR Conversation Model

C—Check In: "How are you doing? How's your workload feeling?"

L—Link to Purpose: "I want to talk about X because I care about your success and our team's success."

E—Explore Together: "Can you help me understand what happened with [specific situation]?"

A—Align on Solutions: "What do you think needs to change? What support do you need?"

R—Reinforce and Follow Up: "Let's meet again on [date] to see how this is going."

Power Questions for Tough Conversations

For ownership:

- "What's your take on how things went?"
- "How do you think this situation affected [others/project/goals]?"
- "What do you wish you had done differently?"

For problem-solving:

- "What obstacles are you facing that I might not be aware of?"
- "What would need to change for this to go smoothly next time?"
- "What kind of support would be most helpful?"

For commitment:

- "What are you willing to commit to moving forward?"
- "How will we both know you're making progress?"

- "What should I do if I see this pattern continuing?"

Follow-Up Framework

Week 1: Check-in via email or brief conversation

Week 2: More detailed progress discussion

Week 3: Formal evaluation of improvement

If needed: Escalate to formal performance planning

Your Tough Conversation Challenge

Identify one person who needs a tough conversation that you've been avoiding:

1. **Use the preconversation checklist** to prepare.
2. **Schedule the conversation** within the next week.
3. **Apply the CLEAR model** during the discussion.
4. **Set specific follow-up dates** before you end the meeting.
5. **Document the key points** and commitments made.

Remember: The longer you wait, the harder it gets. Your team—and the person who needs the feedback—is counting on you to lead with courage and clarity.

CHAPTER 8

HANDLING RESISTANCE LIKE A PRO

You've mastered tough conversations. You know how to put the cognitive load on your team and create ownership through dialogue. But what happens when people don't just struggle to meet expectations—they actively resist them?

Welcome to one of leadership's most frustrating challenges: dealing with pushback, excuses, and resistance. This is where many leaders lose their nerve. They start making exceptions, accepting explanations, and hoping things will improve. But here's the truth: **When you tolerate resistance, you teach it.**

The good news? Resistance isn't personal; it's predictable. And when you know what to expect, you can handle it like a pro.

THE FOUNDATION: DON'T TOLERATE EXCUSES

One of the most important things I do to eliminate excuses, resistance, and pushback is simple: I don't tolerate it. I make it clear from the start that our organization has a set of values and operating principles, and one of those principles is that we don't make excuses here. I also make it clear that high performers don't make excuses; they take full responsibility. Period. The best people own their outcomes, good or bad, and they find solutions instead of justifying failure or mediocrity.

Managing the narrative is a critical part of shaping the culture of any team or organization. Just as it's important to define who we are and what we stand for, it's just as powerful, if not more powerful, to define who we are not. Saying things like "We don't accept mediocrity" or "We don't push back just for the sake of pushing back" helps eliminate the kind of resistance that derails progress.

When that clarity is present, pushback that does arise tends to be focused and productive. It's not about personal preference or discomfort with change. It's about improving systems, sharpening execution, and advancing results.

CASE STUDY: WHEN EXCUSES MEET ACCOUNTABILITY

A powerful example of this came when I was supporting a school leader named Principal Lewis. She had inherited a seventh-grade classroom that had become a chronic source of chaos and complaints. Students were disengaged. Parents were calling. Walk-through data was abysmal. And the teacher, Ms. Carter, always had a justification.

Trauma. Student behavior. Tools that didn't work. Support staff who didn't show up. Every conversation was met with another reason why the classroom was failing. Never once did she take full ownership.

One morning, after walking into the classroom and observing pure disorder before the first bell even rang, Principal Lewis had seen enough. That afternoon, they sat down for a conversation.

"I know what you're going to say," Ms. Carter began. "But these kids come in with so much trauma. They're not ready to learn. The walk-through tool doesn't capture what I'm trying to do. And I had to scrap my lesson plan yesterday because the para didn't show up."

Principal Lewis responded calmly, directly. "Ms. Carter, I hear you. But in this building, we don't make excuses. We don't lower the bar because things are hard. We create systems to meet the bar in spite of the challenges."

She then handed Ms. Carter a document: the Criteria for Success (CFS) they had aligned on in August. Daily objectives. Routines in place by 8:00 a.m. Student engagement above 80 percent. They had discussed it. Reviewed it. Supported it. And it had not been followed.

"This isn't about your talent," Lewis told her. "I've seen your best. But when we normalize chaos, kids suffer. And when you operate out of alignment with our expectations, you impact everyone else around you."

By the end of the quarter, Ms. Carter made the choice to step away from the role. There was no drama, no fallout. Just a recognition that it wasn't the right fit. A teaching fellow, who had been groomed and prepped to take over midyear, stepped in. Within weeks, the students began to thrive. Routines improved. Learning became visible. And the culture of the grade level stabilized.

This story illustrates why mantras, values, and consistent reinforcement matter. When an organization builds a culture of clarity and responsibility, people internalize those expectations. They begin to understand not just what is expected but what is not tolerated.

THE POWER OF CRITERIA FOR SUCCESS (CFS)

Another key way to eliminate excuses before they start is setting a clear Criteria for Success from the outset. It serves as a tool for alignment, coaching, and accountability throughout any initiative. Too often, leaders hold a vision of success in their heads and communicate it loosely. Then, when a team member returns with a product that misses the mark, there's frustration and confusion.

The CFS solves this problem. It removes ambiguity. When expectations are crystal clear, excuses have no place to hide. That was the case in room 104. Principal Lewis didn't just hope for structure. She had defined what it looked like, reviewed it, and followed up. So when performance faltered, there was no confusion, only clarity.

When combined with consistent follow-up, regular coaching, and adequate support, clear expectations create a culture where people either rise to the standard or self-select out. No one can say they didn't know. And no one can pretend they weren't given the tools to succeed.

UNDERSTANDING THE THREE TYPES OF RESISTANCE

Not all resistance is created equal. Understanding what you're dealing with helps you respond appropriately:

TYPE 1: LEGITIMATE CONCERNS

This is productive pushback. Someone raises genuine questions about resources, timeline, or feasibility. They're not resisting for the sake of resisting; they're trying to make the work better.

How to handle it: Listen, evaluate, and incorporate good ideas. "That's a great point about timing. Let's think through how to address that."

TYPE 2: CHANGE AVERSION

This person isn't against the goal; they're uncomfortable with change. They might say things like, "We've always done it this way" or "I'm not sure this will work with our students."

How to handle it: Acknowledge their experience, connect to values, and provide support. "I know this feels different from what you're used to. Let's talk about how this aligns with our commitment to student success."

TYPE 3: FUNDAMENTAL MISALIGNMENT

This person consistently resists, makes excuses, and pushes back regardless of the issue. Like Ms. Carter, they're not aligned with the culture or expectations.

How to handle it: Clear boundaries, documented conversations, and ultimately transition planning if needed.

THE RESPONSE STRATEGY: STAY CALM, STAY CLEAR

When resistance shows up, here's your approach:

STEP 1: LISTEN FIRST

Don't immediately shut down pushback. Sometimes there's valuable information hidden in the resistance. "Help me understand your concern."

STEP 2: ACKNOWLEDGE, DON'T VALIDATE

You can acknowledge someone's feelings without agreeing with their position. "I hear that you're frustrated. And I also need you to understand that this expectation isn't negotiable."

STEP 3: REDIRECT TO SOLUTIONS

Move the conversation from problems to solutions. "Given that this is our direction, what would help you be successful with it?"

STEP 4: REINFORCE THE STANDARD

Bring it back to your values and expectations. "Remember, we're a team that finds solutions, not excuses. How can we make this work?"

WHEN SOMEONE ISN'T IN THE RIGHT SEAT

At the end of the day, when people consistently push back, resist, or make excuses, it's often a sign that they're in the wrong role, or the wrong organization altogether. One of the most important responsibilities of a leader is knowing their team. That includes understanding their strengths and potential but also recognizing their limitations.

When leaders take the time to assess team members deeply, they can often realign underperformers into roles where they're more likely to thrive. And sometimes, that role isn't within the organization at all, and that's okay.

When Ms. Carter left, it wasn't a punishment. It was a recognition that she was no longer thriving. People who are struggling to meet expectations, resisting accountability, and constantly pushing back are likely unhappy. They feel out of alignment, and they know they aren't succeeding.

When leaders avoid these conversations and let underperformance continue, everyone suffers: the individual, the team, the culture, and ultimately, the organization's outcomes.

THE CULTURE YOU CREATE

Here's what happens when you handle resistance consistently and fairly:

- **Your best people respect you** because they see that standards matter.
- **Chronic resisters either improve or leave** because they can't hide behind excuses.
- **The team focuses on solutions** instead of problems.
- **Change becomes easier** because people know resistance won't derail progress.
- **Performance improves** because energy goes toward execution, not pushback.

MOVING FORWARD WITH CONFIDENCE

Handling resistance isn't about being harsh or inflexible. It's about being clear, consistent, and committed to your values. When you set the standard that excuses aren't acceptable and follow through with support and accountability, you create a culture where people either rise up or self-select out.

And that's exactly what you want.

Avoidance is not leadership. Hope is not a strategy.

Leaders must be clear. They must be direct. And they must be willing to have the tough conversations. Because when they do, everyone benefits.

You've now mastered tough conversations and learned to handle resistance with confidence. But here's the ultimate test of accountability leadership: Can you hold yourself to the same standards you set for your team? The most credible leaders don't just demand accountability; they model it.

TOOL KIT: YOUR GAME PLAN FOR PUSHBACK

Ready to handle resistance like a pro? Use these tools to address pushback while maintaining relationships and standards.

The Resistance Decoder: Identifying What You're Really Dealing With

Legitimate Concerns Sound Like:

- "I'm worried we don't have enough time for this."
- "What if parents have questions about this change?"
- "I think we might need additional training first."

Change Aversion Sounds Like:

- "We've always done it this way."
- "I'm not comfortable with this approach."
- "This won't work with our population."

Fundamental Misalignment Sounds Like:

- "This is ridiculous."
- "Nobody asked me what I thought."
- "I shouldn't have to do this."

The CALM Response Method

When facing resistance, stay **CALM**:

C—Clarify: "Help me understand your specific concern."

A—Acknowledge: "I can see this feels overwhelming."

L—Link: "Let's connect this back to our goal of [specific outcome]."

M—Move Forward: "Given our direction, what support do you need to make this successful?"

Power Phrases for Common Resistance

For Excuse Making:

- "I hear you naming challenges. What solutions are you considering?"
- "Help me understand what you're going to do differently moving forward."
- "We're a team that finds ways to make things work. What's your plan?"

For Change Resistance:

- "I know change can feel uncomfortable. Our commitment to [value] means we need to try this."
- "What would help you feel more confident about this transition?"
- "Let's focus on how this serves our students/mission/goals."

For Fundamental Pushback:

- "This expectation isn't negotiable. Let's talk about how to make it work."
- "I need to be clear: This is our direction. How can I support your success with it?"
- "We've made this decision based on our values. What questions do you have about implementation?"

Creating Your Criteria for Success (CFS)

For any major initiative or expectation, create a CFS document that includes:

What Success Looks Like:

- Specific, observable behaviors
- Measurable outcomes

- Timeline for implementation

Support Provided:

- Training offered
- Resources available
- Check-in schedule

How Progress Will Be Measured:

- Data points to track
- Observation criteria
- Feedback timeline

Next Steps If Standards Aren't Met:

- Additional support plan
- Timeline for improvement
- Escalation process

Your Resistance Action Plan

- **Step 1:** Identify one person who consistently pushes back or makes excuses.
- **Step 2:** Determine which type of resistance you're dealing with using the decoder.
- **Step 3:** Plan your response using the CALM method.
- **Step 4:** Have the conversation using your power phrases.
- **Step 5:** Create a CFS document if expectations aren't clear.
- **Step 6:** Follow up within one week to reinforce expectations.

Remember: The Goal Isn't to Eliminate All Pushback

Healthy organizations have productive dialogue and disagreement. The goal is to eliminate:

- Excuse making that prevents accountability
- Resistance that derails progress
- Pushback that undermines team morale

When you handle resistance skillfully, you create space for the right kind of feedback while maintaining your standards. That's leadership.

CHAPTER 9

LEADING BY EXAMPLE

THE ACCOUNTABILITY MIRROR

You've learned to have tough conversations and handle resistance like a pro. But here's the ultimate test of your accountability leadership: Can you hold yourself to the same standards you set for your team?

This is where many leaders lose credibility without even realizing it. They demand excellence from others while making excuses for themselves. They expect preparation from their team while winging their own presentations. They ask for feedback to be received gracefully while getting defensive when someone questions their decisions.

The most effective leaders hold themselves to the same standards they set for their teams. They don't just talk about values, expectations, and execution—they live them. Accountability isn't something you demand from others; it's something you embody.

When leaders fall short on this, they lose credibility, erode trust, and send the message that "Do as I say, not as I do" is acceptable. But when you model accountability, you set the tone for the entire organization—and you make it clear that the expectations apply at every level.

THE MIRROR STARTS WITH YOU

If you expect your team to rehearse and prepare, you have to do it too—and do it visibly. That's leadership. You can't ask others to meet a bar you're unwilling to reach yourself. And people aren't just listening to what you say; they're watching what you do.

This chapter is about the mirror: the reflection your team sees every time you show up, follow through, or fall short. Leadership is personal. It's not about being perfect; it's about being aligned. If you want accountability to stick, you have to live it out loud.

SETTING THE STANDARD: THE POWER OF PRACTICING WHAT YOU PREACH

One of the best examples of how I held myself to the same standard I expected from my team was through modeling morning meeting expectations. Leading a powerful, engaging morning meeting became one of my biggest strengths—not because I was naturally gifted at it, but because I practiced relentlessly.

Our school became known for having some of the best morning meetings in the city, arguably in the state. But that didn't happen by accident. It happened because I was willing to do the work behind the scenes, just like I expected my staff to do.

Every single time I was scheduled to lead a morning meeting, I arrived early to practice. I didn't just glance at my notes or mentally run through my slides; I went all in. I stood in the empty auditorium, pulled up my presentation, and delivered the meeting as if the students and staff were in front of me. When it came time for our signature call to attention, where we would yell "Gooooooood mooorning, DSST!" at full volume, I did it with the same energy and enthusiasm I would bring in front of my students and staff.

And the best part? My teachers, staff, and leaders could hear me. They heard me practicing. They saw that I wasn't just expecting them to prepare and rehearse; I was doing it myself.

I was sending a very clear message:

1. **At this school, we practice before we execute.** Excellence doesn't happen by accident. We believe in preparation, refinement, and building muscle memory through repetition.
2. **No one has "arrived"—including me.** It doesn't matter how long you've been teaching, leading, or how much of an expert you are, you still have to practice to get better. Growth is nonnegotiable.
3. **Humility and mastery go hand in hand.** Being great at something doesn't mean you stop working at it. True excellence comes from constantly pushing to improve.

That moment—me standing alone in a room, rehearsing, pushing myself to model the level of effort and preparation I expected from my team—set a standard. I was leading by example.

THE RIPPLE EFFECT: WHEN MODELING CREATES CULTURE

Soon after, I started noticing a shift. Teachers began staying late the night before their own grade-level or content team meetings. They were printing out agendas, rehearsing their facilitation, double-checking timing. Some of them even asked for feedback on their delivery.

They were modeling the same behavior I'd been showing them, without me ever asking.

That's when I realized something important: My preparation

didn't just set a bar. It gave permission. It made preparation feel normal. It created a culture where excellence wasn't just expected; it was owned.

The mirror I held up to my team started with me. They didn't just hear me talk about preparation; they saw me live it. That's how cultures of accountability are built: not with policies, but with examples.

HOW THE LEADERSHIP MIRROR SUPPORTS THE VERB FRAMEWORK

When you model accountability consistently, you strengthen every component of the VERB framework:

- **Values First:** Your actions demonstrate what the values actually look like in practice, making them real rather than abstract.
- **Expectations Clear:** When you meet your own expectations visibly, you show that standards apply to everyone, eliminating the "rules for thee but not for me" dynamic.
- **Real Progress:** You track and share your own progress, showing that growth and improvement are ongoing for everyone.
- **Buy-In and Ownership:** People are more likely to own expectations they see you owning yourself. Your modeling creates permission for excellence.

FIVE STRATEGIES FOR HOLDING YOURSELF ACCOUNTABLE—PUBLICLY

The key to effective self-accountability is doing it visibly. Your team needs to see that you hold yourself to the same standards you set for them. Here are five strategies you can implement immediately:

1. PUBLICLY COMMIT TO YOUR OWN STANDARDS

If you expect your team to submit reports on time, show up to meetings prepared, or continuously develop their skills, make sure you're doing the same. Share your personal commitments and goals with your team so they see that accountability isn't just for them; it's for you, too.

Example: "I'm committing to responding to all emails within twenty-four hours, just like I expect from you. If I miss that standard, please call me out on it."

2. ASK FOR FEEDBACK—AND ACT ON IT

Create a culture where your team feels comfortable giving you honest feedback. If you expect employees to improve based on feedback, you must demonstrate that you're willing to do the same.

Set up structured ways to gather input: surveys, one-to-one check-ins, leadership reviews. Most importantly, show that you take their insights seriously by making visible changes and telling them about it. And don't forget to thank them for their feedback.

Example: "Based on your feedback that I was rushing through meetings, I've restructured our agenda to include more discussion time. How does this feel?"

3. OWN YOUR MISTAKES—LOUDLY AND CLEARLY

Great leaders make mistakes, but they don't make excuses. If you miss a deadline, make a bad decision, or fall short on an expectation, acknowledge it openly.

Saying "I dropped the ball on this, and here's how I'm fixing it" models exactly what you expect from your team when they fall short. Apologize if your mistake negatively impacted someone in your sphere of influence.

Example: "I completely missed our deadline for the budget review, and I know that affected your planning. That's on me. Here's what I'm doing to make sure it doesn't happen again."

4. MEASURE YOUR OWN PERFORMANCE

Just like you track team goals and outcomes, you should have your own system for tracking your progress. Set specific leadership targets (e.g., coaching a certain number of staff per month, improving communication, or strengthening decision-making) and hold yourself accountable to hitting them.

Share your progress with your team as appropriate.

Example: "My goal was to have meaningful one-on-ones with each of you monthly. I hit that target with eight out of ten of you in November. I'm adjusting my calendar to make sure I don't miss anyone in December."

5. CREATE AN ACCOUNTABILITY PARTNER OR PEER CHECK-IN SYSTEM

Even the best leaders need support with accountability. Find another leader, inside or outside of your organization, who will challenge you to stay aligned with your own values and commitments.

Regular check-ins with someone who isn't afraid to call you out when you slip up can keep you sharp and ensure that you're leading by example.

THE TEN-MINUTE LEADERSHIP MOVE THAT CHANGES CULTURE

Here's one of the simplest, most powerful modeling moves I've ever seen—and it didn't involve a live presentation, a speech, or even a conversation. Just an email.

My boss noticed we needed to be more intentional as a

senior leadership team—more thoughtful about planning our year, mapping out goals, aligning milestones, and structuring our weekly cadence with purpose. Instead of micromanaging or nitpicking individual plans, he did something brilliant.

He created his own planning document, but he made sure it was nothing short of excellent. Every part of it modeled what he wanted to see. Clear goals. Detailed timelines. A week-by-week focus on priorities and relationships.

And then, right before planning season began, he sent it out.

The email was short: "Hey, here's an example of my planning doc. Feel free to take it and use it as-is or tweak it. If you do use it, let me know how it goes."

That's it. No fuss. Just a clean, clear, well-timed model.

And it worked. The ripple effect was immediate. As plans came in from across the team, you could see his influence everywhere— either exact replications or strong adaptations. It raised the bar, quietly but completely. And it took maybe ten minutes of his time.

Sometimes modeling isn't about standing in front of the room. It's about building something strong enough to be worth emulating, and then sharing it at just the right moment.

THE CULTURE YOU CREATE

When leaders commit to holding themselves accountable first, it creates an environment where accountability is respected, not resented. When you lead with consistency, clarity, and ownership, your team follows suit—not because they're told to, but because they've seen what it looks like.

Your actions set the cultural standard far more than your words ever could. If you want a culture of ownership, trust, and execution, start by looking in the mirror.

The leadership mirror reflects more than your individual performance; it reflects the standards your entire organization will embrace. Make sure what your team sees is worth following.

TOOL KIT: LEADING BY AN EXAMPLE THAT INSPIRES

Ready to become the leader your team wants to follow? Use these tools to hold yourself accountable and model the standards you expect from others.

The Mirror Assessment: Where Do You Stand?

Rate yourself honestly (1–5 scale) in each area:

- **Preparation:** Do you prepare for meetings/presentations as thoroughly as you expect your team to? _____
- **Timeliness:** Do you meet deadlines and arrive on time consistently? _____
- **Communication:** Do you respond to emails/messages within your stated time frame? _____
- **Feedback Reception:** Do you receive feedback gracefully and act on it visibly? _____
- **Mistake Ownership:** Do you acknowledge errors openly and take responsibility? _____
- **Growth Mindset:** Do you actively seek learning opportunities and show vulnerability? _____
- **Follow-Through:** Do you do what you say you'll do, when you said you'd do it? _____

Your lowest score is your starting point for modeling improvement.

The Visible Accountability Plan

Step 1: Pick Your Focus—Choose one behavior you want your team to improve. Ask yourself: "How well do I model this myself?"

Step 2: Make It Public—Share a specific commitment with your team: "I'm going to [specific behavior] and I want you to hold me accountable."

Step 3: Track and Share—Create a simple system to track your progress and report back to your team regularly.

Step 4: Own Your Misses—When you fall short, acknowledge it quickly and specifically with your team.

Step 5: Celebrate Growth—Share what you're learning and how feedback is helping you improve.

Power Phrases for Self-Accountability

When Sharing Your Commitments:

- "I'm going to hold myself to the same standard I expect from all of you."
- "Here's what I'm working on personally, and I'd appreciate your feedback."
- "I want to model what I'm asking you to do."

When Asking for Feedback:

- "What's one thing I could do differently to support your success?"
- "I want to get better at [specific skill]. What have you noticed?"
- "Help me understand how my [behavior] affects your work."

When Owning Mistakes:

- "I dropped the ball on [specific situation]. Here's how I'm fixing it."
- "I didn't handle [situation] well. What I should have done is [specific behavior]."
- "I fell short of my own standard here. I'm going to [specific action] to improve."

The Reflection Practice: Modeling What Matters

Use this five-minute reflection weekly:

1. **Identify the behavior:** What's one behavior you want to see more of in your team?
2. **Take inventory:** How have you modeled this behavior both implicitly (just doing it) and explicitly (demonstrating it purposefully)?
3. **Look for the gap:** Where have you asked for this behavior without modeling it fully yourself?
4. **Make it visible:** What's one small way you can model this behavior more clearly this week?
5. **Create shared reflection:** Where can you invite your team to reflect on this behavior together without making it about compliance?

Your Modeling Challenge

This week, pick one area where you want to strengthen your modeling:

☐ **Preparation:** Practice/prepare for something your team can observe.

☐ **Vulnerability:** Share a mistake and what you learned from it.

☐ **Growth:** Ask for specific feedback and act on it visibly.

☐ **Standards:** Publicly commit to meeting an expectation you have for others.

☐ **Follow-through:** Do something you said you'd do, and let people know you did it.

Remember: The goal isn't perfection—it's alignment. Your team needs to see you living the values and expectations you've set, especially when it's challenging.

The mirror reflects what you do far more powerfully than what you say. Make sure your reflection is worth following.

CONCLUSION

ACCOUNTABILITY WINS

You've been on quite a journey. You started by shifting your mindset about what accountability really means—discovering it's not about punishment or micromanagement, but about clarity, support, and empowerment. You've learned to navigate tough conversations, handle resistance like a pro, and hold yourself to the same standards you set for others.

You've seen Sarah struggle without accountability systems, watched Darien learn to lead with purpose instead of power, and witnessed how clear expectations transformed a chaotic classroom into a thriving learning environment. You've discovered that a simple quarterly air filter change can create better tenant relationships and that practicing your morning meeting alone in an empty auditorium can shift an entire school's culture.

At this point, you have everything you need to shift your mindset, transform your leadership, and build a culture of real accountability.

Here's what it comes down to: **Hope is not a strategy.**

Waiting, wishing, or assuming people will execute without a structured system will only lead to inconsistency, frustration, and missed opportunities. The best teams, and the best leaders, don't operate on hope. They operate on clarity, consistency, and ownership.

Despite popular belief, accountability has never been about micromanagement. It's about setting a high bar, being crystal clear about expectations, modeling exactly what you expect, and being relentless about progress monitoring, support, and follow-through. It's about creating a culture where *everyone* owns the outcome.

THE FRAMEWORK THAT CHANGES EVERYTHING

You now have a blueprint. The **VERB framework** isn't just a series of steps to follow. It's a way of thinking, leading, and building culture:

Values First: Anchor everything in what matters most. Values that aren't reinforced are just decoration. Values in action are culture.

Expectations Clear: Leave zero room for interpretation. Make it so clear they'd have to *try* to get it wrong.

Real Progress: Inspect what you expect. Follow-up isn't micromanagement; it's leadership.

Buy-In and Ownership: Get your team to want what you want. That's how you stop chasing people and start empowering them.

When these four components work together, something powerful happens. Excuses disappear. Trust builds. Performance improves. Culture strengthens. Your best people stay because they're part of something they believe in, and accountability becomes something your team embraces rather than endures.

GO FORTH AND LEAD DIFFERENTLY

The truth is that most leaders don't fail because of bad intentions. They fail because they haven't established a culture of accountability and don't have a system to ensure follow-through. That's no longer your problem.

You've seen the stories. You've learned the tools. You've reflected on the mistakes and recognized the patterns. You know what happens when leaders lead with clarity and when they don't. You understand the cost of avoiding tough conversations and the power of putting cognitive load on your team. You've witnessed how modeling excellence creates permission for others to excel.

But here's the reality: Knowledge without action is just expensive entertainment.

YOUR STARTING POINT

Don't let this book sit on a shelf. Don't try to implement everything at once. Instead, pick your starting point:

If your challenge is unclear expectations: Start with Chapter 4. Pick one critical expectation that isn't being met consistently. Define exactly what success looks like, create your Criteria for Success document, and make it so clear your team would have to *try* to get it wrong.

If your challenge is avoiding tough conversations: Start with Chapter 7. Identify one person who needs feedback you've been putting off. Use the CLEAR conversation model and put the cognitive load on them by asking instead of telling.

If your challenge is team resistance: Start with Chapter 8. Use the resistance decoder to identify what type of pushback you're dealing with, then apply the CALM response method to address it without compromising your standards.

If your challenge is modeling accountability: Start with Chapter 9. Choose one behavior you expect from your team and commit to modeling it visibly for the next thirty days.

If you're ready for the full system: Start with Chapter 3. Define your core values and the behaviors that bring them to life. This foundation will make everything else more powerful.

THE CHOICE IS YOURS

You have two paths ahead of you.

You can be the leader who waits, hoping things improve—the one who sets expectations but doesn't follow through, who avoids hard conversations until they become crises, who manages by exception instead of building systems for success.

Or, you can be the leader who drives real impact—the one who creates clarity instead of confusion, who builds accountability instead of hoping for compliance, who transforms cultures through consistent, values-driven leadership.

The difference between these two leaders isn't talent, experience, or charisma. It's using systems. It's follow-through. It's the courage to hold the line on what matters most.

Your team is watching. They're waiting to see which leader you'll choose to be. They want clear expectations. They crave feedback that helps them grow. They're hoping you'll create the kind of culture where excellence isn't accidental, it's inevitable.

Many are counting on you. Your team members who want to do great work but need clearer direction. Your organization that needs the kind of leadership that builds something sustainable and transformative.

THE TIME IS NOW

Teams don't change with time. They change with leadership. And leadership isn't about waiting for the perfect moment or having all the answers. It's about taking the next right step with clarity and conviction.

So what will you do with what you've learned?

Go forward. Lead boldly. Set the bar high. Follow through. Hold yourself and others accountable.

Start this week. Pick one thing. Do it well. Build from there.

Because at the end of the day, accountability wins.

And now, so will you.

THANK YOU FOR READING

You made it to the end—and that says everything about your commitment to leadership.

Writing this book has been a labor of love, born from years of working alongside incredible educators and leaders who refuse to accept mediocrity. Every story, every framework, every tool in these pages comes from real experience in real schools with real challenges.

Thank you for your commitment to excellence. Thank you for the work you do every day. And thank you for taking the time to invest in your leadership.

You have my full support.

—Brandi Nicole Chin
(Coach Chin)

A QUICK FAVOR

Please take two minutes to rate this book on Amazon.

I love feedback and hearing from my readers. Your feedback will help me to generate new ideas for future books and resources. When you share your honest review, you help other principals, superintendents, and education leaders discover tools that could transform their schools and teams.

Whether this book challenged your thinking, gave you practical tools, or simply reminded you why this work matters, I want to hear about it. Your voice helps shape how these ideas reach other leaders who need them.

Your review makes a difference.

JOIN THE WEEKLY LEADERSHIP HUDDLE

Because great leaders never stop learning.

Throughout my career, I've had the privilege of learning from the very best in education and leadership: principals who transformed struggling schools, superintendents who built thriving networks, and coaches who developed exceptional leaders. This field has given me everything, and now it's my turn to pay it forward.

Every week, I send out a leadership email huddle packed with:

- **Real strategies** from high-performing schools and organizations
- **Practical tools** you can implement immediately
- **Mindset shifts** that separate good leaders from great ones
- **Stories and case studies** from the field that will challenge your thinking

These are the same insights I share with the school and network leaders I coach. Whether you're a first-year principal or a seasoned superintendent, these weekly huddles will sharpen your leadership edge and keep you connected to what's working in our field.

Scan the following QR code to join us at www.coachchin.com.

SCAN ME

PS: I also work with a small group of high-potential, high-performing school and network leaders through intensive coaching and professional development. If you're interested in exploring this kind of partnership, reach out to me at brandi@ coachchin.com.

Hope Is Not a Strategy: The Huddle (Where Accountability Meets Action)

ACKNOWLEDGMENTS

To my husband, Fabian Chin, my anchor and my rock: You are the steady force behind me, the one I can always trust and rely on through every high and low. Your presence is a gift from God, and I wouldn't be the leader I am today without your unwavering belief in me. Thank you for every act of love, large and small. I love you deeply and endlessly.

To my mother, Denise Wilson: Your resilience and determination taught me that where there is a will, there is always a way. Because of you, I move through the world with a strong sense of self.

To my children, Ari, Maddie, and Ash. Ari, your light inspires me to be the best version of myself. You remind me to lead with joy, stay grounded in the present, and let my brilliance shine. You fill my life with love. Maddie and Ash, you've taught me the power of intention and manifestation and have always believed in me.

To Bill Kurtz: Your leadership, grounded in values and humanity, profoundly shaped who I am. You have my deepest respect and admiration. Your example of excellence and empathy continues to influence how I lead and live.

To Doug Lemov: Thank you for being an early believer. You've always held the bar high and I've grown because of your example.

To Eric Scroggins: Thank you for being a bold and generous leader who truly sees people. Your consistent support and belief in me have meant the world. The law of giving is alive in you, and it's no surprise you're among the best in our field.

To Alexis Ulaj and Brandon Sorlie, my accountability partners, thought partners, and coconspirators in bringing this book to life: Thank you for walking beside me and for allowing your stories to inspire others.

And to God, my source, my center, my everything: Your grace, mercy, and unconditional love renew me daily. I am forever grateful and I give You all the glory.

ABOUT THE AUTHOR

DR. BRANDI NICOLE CHIN is a nationally recognized expert in educational leadership with over sixteen years of experience transforming schools that serve marginalized communities. Her work has been published in *Education Week* and *The Denver Post* and featured in *Teach like a Champion 2.0* and Relay Graduate School's Follow the Leaders series.

Dr. Chin leads strategic initiatives to expand high-quality school options throughout the greater St. Louis region and across Missouri. She previously served as assistant superintendent at Uncommon Schools and was founding school director of DSST Middle School at Noel Campus, where she led the school to become the number one school in Denver, achieving the highest academic growth in the city and second-highest in the state.

Dr. Chin has coached hundreds of school leaders nationwide through Relay's National Principals Academy Fellowship and through her own consulting practice. An entrepreneur, she co-owns a real estate investment company with both active and passive investments in more than 850 units worth $152 million.

She holds a PhD in education policy with a cognate in statistics from the University of Denver, a BGS from the University of Michigan, and a master's degree in K–12 education from Regis University. She lives in St. Charles, Missouri, with her family.

www.ingramcontent.com/pod-product-compliance
Lightning Source LLC
Chambersburg PA
CBHW030526210326
41597CB00013B/1040